MOUNTAIN
WATER

MOUNTAIN
WATER

*The Way of the
High-Country Angler*

CRAIG MARTIN

PRUETT PUBLISHING
BOULDER, COLORADO
1999

Printed in the United States

08 07 06 05 04 03 02 01 00 99   5 4 3 2 1

Library of Congress Cataloging-in-Publication Data

Martin, Craig, 1952–
    Mountain water : the way of the high-country angler / Craig Martin.
      p. cm.
    ISBN 0-87108-896-7 (alk. paper)
    1. Trout fishing. 2. Fly fishing. I. Title.
    SH687.M2985 1999
    799.1'24—dc21   99-037861
                                                CIP

Cover and book design by Paulette Livers Lambert
Book composition by Lyn Chaffee
Illustrations by Rod Walinchus
Cover and interior photographs by Craig Martin

*To Jessica and Alex, in anticipation of
summer days to come,
spent in the high country*

CONTENTS

ACKNOWLEDGMENTS

This book is rooted in several summers of fly-fishing trips into the mountains of Colorado with Kevin Ott, who introduced me to fly fishing under mountain-water rules and to whom special thanks are due. Discussions with Jan Crawford, Bill Orr, and Karen Denison of the High Desert Angler in Santa Fe helped refine the concept of mountain water. Thanks to Manuel Monasterio of the Reel Life in Albuquerque for listening to me and for providing a forum to test my ideas on mountain angling; to New Mexico Trout and the Sangre de Cristo Fly Fishers, who offered opportunities to hear how other anglers felt about the simplification of fly fishing; to Tom Knopick and John Flick of Duranglers in Durango, who opened up my eyes to more than a few mountain-water techniques; to Van Beacham of the Solitary Angler for his insights on pocket water; to Dave Hughes, one of the sensible voices in modern angling literature, for validating my excitement and pleasure in hauling in a 5-inch cutthroat trout; to Marykay Cicio of Pruett Publishing for getting this book started on the right foot and to Kim Adams for seeing it through its completion; to my wife, June Fabryka-Martin, for putting up with the years when size and quantity of trout were more important than the quality of the experience; and to my children, Jessica and Alex, for bringing more smiles to my face than the trout we pull out of the mountain water.

An earlier version of chapter five, Picking Pockets, appeared in the March 1996 issue of *Fly Fisherman*; the lightning section of chapter one first appeared as "Bolts from the Blue" in the July/August 1998 issue of *American Angler*; and a longer version of Stream of Consciousness, a section in chapter nine, appeared in the 1994 spring issue of the *Flyfisher*.

INTRODUCTION

Fly Fishing for the Rest of Us

I f you've read even a fraction of the prolific hatch of fly-fishing books and magazines available to the angler, or if you've ever hired an experienced guide to show you the ropes of some special water, you know there are a lot of lucky people out there. As fly fishing reaches for the mainstream, an increasing number of authors and guides make their living by fishing, and due to the nature of the business, they must spend most of their days on the water, fly rod in hand, practicing the art of the sport we know and love so well.

The rest of us fantasize about joining the ranks of those fortunate enough to call fishing "work." We are "regular" people who rarely get to spend more than a few precious summer weekends on our favorite waters. I know that's the way it is with me. If I spend parts of thirty days a year fly fishing, it's a good year. Because of family, work, and other obligations, I'm forced to squeeze what fishing I can into a few hours on Sunday, and occasionally I sneak off for a day in the middle of the week.

My time on the water is limited, and I therefore make a host of demands on my fishing experiences. That makes me rather particular about where I fish, and that's why I go out of my way to seek mountain water—that glorious landscape found most often above 6,000 feet that offers the angler solitude, different types of challenges, and unspeakable beauty. In forests of Douglas fir and spruce, in rough-and-tumble canyons, in alpine meadows, and in mirror-surfaced glacial lakes, I find the secret places that most anglers pass by on their way to some famous pool that is renowned for its legendary trout.

In these headwaters, I know I won't scare up large trout, nor will I find trout aplenty. But I will have the opportunity to practice a visual, active, traditional type of fly fishing. Certainly mountain water can be described in terms of place—subalpine forests, timberline meadows, rugged canyons—but in reality, it is better defined as a style of fly fishing. Mountain water is anyplace where success in angling relies on technique and knowledge of trout habits rather than on the equipment and fly pattern you select.

As you might expect, mountain water is most often found in thundering gorges, idyllic high-country parks, and timberline lakes, but such free-flowing water can show up in surprising places. Whether it lies in a sheer-walled canyon amid sagebrush plains, a stair-step brook in deciduous forests, or in a remote glade in Appalachian hills, mountain water means wild water, wild country, and wild trout.

Angling mountain water is a throwback to the fly-fishing style of old. It's simply the angler, the water, and the trout that count. Fly fishing mountain water is full of fun rather than finesse because it's so visual. These are the skills discussed in this book. You must search a bit to find fish. You must study the patterns of rock and current. Fly patterns are big and bushy and easy to see, and there is a constant rush of anticipation as you watch a fly bob along the surface. The sight of a trout appearing suddenly from a hidden lie and hammering a fly on the surface is certain to make you tingle all over. Mountain-water angling is active. To cover the water effectively, you must always be on the move, casting constantly. There's adventure in the act of angling. It takes effort to reach the water and to move along the rugged banks. The successful mountain-water angler is skilled at reading the water (instead of the hatch), at getting by with fewer but more effective flies, at presenting patterns with simple, easy-to-master casting techniques, and at finding out-of-the-way places that see few anglers.

Much of the angling literature of the past ten years has been devoted to esoteric skills, refined techniques, and finesse fly fishing, implying that even the slightest variation from perfect will result in no fish. This is perhaps true because more anglers flock to the thrill of big-fish tailwaters where such attention to detail is necessary. The result, however, is the creation of the false impression that fly fishing is an impossibly complicated sport.

Mountain waters tend to demystify the sport of fly fishing. Micromanaged skills are not required. The fish are forgiving—or at least most of them are. They are willing feeders, and you can get away with a lot of so-called "mistakes." On a mountain stream, a long, graceful cast is worth as much as an American light beer in an English pub. Armed with a couple of the rudimentary skills that are easy to execute and fun to learn, anyone can successfully fish mountain water. It is fly fishing for the common man.

Mountain-Water Rules

In this book, you'll find techniques that will help you put together memorable days fly fishing in valleys, canyons, meadows, and cirques. By understanding five axioms—the mountain-water rules—you'll discover how to catch decent-sized trout in places where most anglers never look twice.

1. *Know how to find trout by reading the water.* To fly fish successfully in mountain water, you have to figure out where the fish are. Whoever coined the term "reading the water" was a wise angler. Like words on a page, the patterns of water movement, foam, and rock tell an important story. If you can read the language of a mountain stream or lake and correctly interpret what is written there, you will be able to find where the trout lie. This is a critical skill, because you rarely see a trout rise on a mountain stream—a much different situation than fishing in more productive, calm water. Most of the time you are forced to find the *spots* where trout are most likely to sit, waiting for food. As you will see, if you find a fish in mountain water, you're apt to get a strike or at least a look. An angler skilled in reading the water will be an effective mountain angler.

   Different types of water read differently, like the various genres of fiction. While the basic skill of finding trout remains the same from stream type to stream type, each *type* of water carries its own patterns and expectations. Most mountain streams are composed of an incredibly complex pattern of moving water. You'll find plenty of advice on how to locate trout in various types of water in the following chapters.

2. *Presentation is often as simple as getting a fly to float in the proper place for two seconds.* Mountain-water angling requires an active approach to the stream. To be successful, you must drift your fly by hundreds of locations a day and have the skills to put the fly where you want it. Presentation on mountain water simply requires that you get the perfect float in the right spot for a brief but perfectly timed interval. Complex currents won't allow long, drag-free drifts no matter how frantically you mend the line. You have to learn easily executed skills that use your rod

more as an extension of your arm rather than as a lever designed to fling a fly long distances. You'll see how to do this in the chapters on freestone and brushy streams and pocket water.

3. *Match the water, not the hatch.* How do you select the proper fly when the fish will take just about anything? Only fly patterns that you can see well and that give you confidence will be effective on mountain water. Understanding this approach to fly selection will make you more successful on the water, permit you to carry fewer flies, and cause you to spend less time at the tying table. Take a close look at chapters three and seven for details about this concept.

4. *Use the simplest tackle and techniques to take fish.* Like all the outdoor-recreation industries, the business of fly fishing thrives on new gear, new technologies, and new materials. But old-fashioned, low-priced rods, reels, flies, and techniques are best suited for mountain water. This type of angling requires that you purchase only a few pieces of good-quality tackle. Chapter two discusses gear and how to strip down what you carry to the essentials.

   Simplification extends to skills, too. On mountain water, you only need to learn how to tie two or three knots well, carry only the flies that you need (not the ones that looked so attractive in a magazine), and invest minimal time mastering simple techniques.

5. *Don't always go for the biggest or most challenging fish. Have fun. Take in the scenery.* If you are the kind of angler who seeks only the challenges of the sport, drop this book as violently as a brown trout spits out a dry fly that's too big. This book doesn't focus on difficult fish—it is concerned with fun, relaxing, scenic fly fishing. Some will say that this is missing the point, that the fun of fly fishing is the challenge. As I see it, many of these anglers lead a vastly

different life than I do. Many of them make their living from angling or are at a different stage of life that permits them the time, the money, and the freedom to pursue the challenges of fly fishing. The rest of us have different priorities, making fly fishing a favorite outdoor pastime—a recreation, plain and simple.

Personally, I would rather backpack with my kids and squeeze in a little fishing time on the side than go off with a buddy and get lost on a river. Thus, most of my time on the water is sandwiched between teaching the kids about trout, camp chores, and strolling the meadows looking for wildlife. Fishing in fits and spurts, I don't often have time to accept a challenge. Rigging up a rod and making a few casts, and letting the tension melt away, is all I have time for. Watching the kids develop a love of the outdoors is far more valuable to me.

Don't get me wrong—there is a time and place for challenging angling. I've fished the Madison, been skunked on the Firehole, and marveled at the red rainbows on the Roaring Fork. But I've learned to take my highest pleasure in the quick grab of a brown trout in swift water, in the pastel palette of a 6-inch brook trout, or in the ripples sent out by a small golden trout that rocks the mirror surface of a glacial lake. Anytime I'm on mountain water, I'm in paradise.

The key to mountain-water fly fishing is that the whole is easier than the sum of its parts. The gestalt of fly fishing—the total experience—is as simple as enjoying time standing in the liquid environment of a trout. There are more ways to succeed than to fail. In fly fishing, the deepest pleasure comes from the simple acts of sport. Casting, studying the intricate patterns of the stream, observing insects, and hanging out in the mountains are their own reward, even on days when the trout are as obvious as hops in a Guinness Stout.

Put the five mountain-water rules to work and you are guaranteed to have glorious days on streams and lakes where few anglers go. You'll still come up empty every now and then, but that won't really matter. You'll still come away feeling on top of the world.

Chapter One

High-Country Safety

Acute Mountain Sickness

Living as I do at 6,343 feet above sea level, it's easy for me to overlook the effects that walking to a mountain stream can have on those who wander in from the flatlands. I've left many a visiting angler gulping for oxygen on what I thought was a stroll to the water, and my photo collection has a subcategory—why most people only go fishing with Craig once.

The foothills of the Jemez Mountains in New Mexico spread from the range like a pleated skirt. Even here on the ruffles, the air is thin—about 75 percent of that on the ocean—but heading up into the high country makes it even more so. In the southern Rockies, there's nary a decent trout stream at 6,000 feet, but head up to 9,000 feet and you'll find some gems. In my stomping grounds in the San Juan Mountains to the north, mountain water is found from 7,000 feet on upward. Even in the northerly confines of Wyoming and Montana, the best mountain streams are still higher than 7,000 feet. In short, angling mountain water means coping with relatively high elevations.

About 50 percent of travelers from sea level to elevations of 8,000 to 12,000 feet suffer from acute mountain sickness (AMS). In its initial phases, AMS is more annoying than a serious health threat. Most people feel a headache, insomnia, fatigue, and a loss of appetite during their first few days at high elevation. Generally, the symptoms go away on their own, but drinking lots of fluids may speed the process. If the symptoms persist, particularly a headache accompanied by nausea, AMS can worsen and become a health threat. Most of the time the symptoms are alleviated by a return to lower elevations. If the symptoms persist, victims should seek medical attention.

The first lesson to be learned about moving about in thinner air is to take it easy. Coming from sea level, don't expect to charge up a trail to reach a special fishing hole. Instead, plan a relaxing pace to get there without gasping for air. Slowing down means limiting your rate of travel to two miles per hour.

Plan some time in your angling schedule to acclimate to higher elevations. Climbers in the Himalayas frequently take a full month to accustom themselves to elevations higher than 18,000 feet; we're talking considerably lower heights here, but the lesson is the same. Spending a day or two at 6,000 feet will make it easier to do what you want to do at 9,000 feet. Despite ten years of living more than a mile high, I still find myself adjusting to anything greater than 10,000 feet. The altitude at which you sleep is more important to your body's adjustment than where you go during the day. So, when I go above 10,000 feet, I never camp more than 1,000 feet higher than the day before.

Dehydration

One of the great paradoxes of angling at high elevation is the threat of dehydration. With all that water around you, it's easy to forget to drink enough fluids. The thin atmosphere holds less water vapor and, when combined with increased exertion, can lead to rapid fluid loss from the body. Even when you don't feel yourself sweating, your body is losing water to the air. By the time you feel thirsty, your body is already at least a quart low on fluids. Proper hydration can help prevent fatigue, headache, and more serious symptoms of altitude sickness. The easy solution is to drink plenty and often. Drink a cup of water before starting out on a day of angling. No—coffee, tea, and alcoholic beverages don't count. Then, drink a cup of water every hour to maintain fluid balance.

Giardia

Those who remember watching Neil Armstrong's first steps on the lunar surface will also recall the Sierra cup and its most pleasant characteristic—the long-handled cup would hang on your belt so that when you were thirsty you simply unhooked the cup, dipped it in the stream, and sucked down the cool, pure water. Alas, you don't see many Sierra cups around these days, because getting a drink from a backcountry stream is no longer so simple.

The spread of the protozoan giardia has put a halt to the dip-and-sip method of rehydrating. This organism is transmitted by cysts that wash from feces of infected mammals. Beaver and cows receive most of the blame for the ubiquitous nature of the disease, but the ever-increasing number of humans in the backcountry is just as much the culprit. Symptoms of infection with giardia begin two days to two weeks from when the organism enters the body. This intestinal disorder causes painful stomach cramps, diarrhea, and nausea. It's not something to be trifled with.

Never drink untreated water from streams or lakes. Treat all water by boiling it for ten minutes or by using chemical tablets to kill all organisms. Water filters are an expensive but convenient alternative, but make certain that you use one with a system that removes large and small organisms.

If you are the cautious type, and perhaps in this case you should be, avoid all contact by mouth with untreated water. Holding a fly line in your mouth qualifies under this broad heading, as does pulling a tippet through your mouth to wet it with saliva before tightening a knot. Keep your fly line in your fingers, and, as uncouth as it may sound, spit on your tippet to lubricate the knots.

Exposure to Ultraviolet Rays

Thin air also offers less protection from the harmful ultraviolet (UV) rays of the sun, so you must protect yourself during a day on the water. This is particularly important because the sun reflects off the surface of the water to intensify the effect for anglers. Remember, too, that cloud cover does nothing to block the UV light, making protection necessary even on cloudy days. The first line of protection is your clothing, so it's a good idea to wear a long-sleeved shirt on the water. Also essential is a wide-brimmed hat, one that will keep the sun off the back of your neck, your ears, and the sides of your face. More protection can be had through the use of sunscreen. Cover your exposed skin—your face, the backs of your hands, your legs, and your ears—with generous amounts of sunscreen at least twice a day. Use a product with a rating of at least 15 SPF.

Weather Changes

In the course of putting this chapter into the computer on this summer afternoon, I've been forced to stop working and turn off the computer three times. The morning began sunny, but then clouds grew over the Jemez Mountains 8 miles away and swelled to eventually block out the sun here in the foothills. Successive waves of rain, along with some impressive lightning, alternated with brilliant blue skies and intense sunshine. Days like this give meaning to the saying, "If you don't like the mountain weather, wait ten minutes and it will change."

Variability and severity of weather changes in the mountains mean that danger from exposure is always hanging over the peaks. Hypothermia, the lowering of the body's core temperature to dangerous levels, is always a threat. In the thin air above 8,000 feet, all it takes is for an angler to be dressed in cotton and then caught in a downpour. Along with the rain comes dropping temperatures. The storms don't always move out quickly, and a long, wet hike back to camp can quickly lead to problems.

The rapidly changing conditions require mountain anglers to *always* carry protection against the weather. Most days on the water will start out warm and sunny, but those conditions rarely last past noon. The only way to maintain comfort and safety is to dress in layers. Start out the day in shorts and a light, synthetic shirt, but keep warmer clothing in the car or in your pack. Fleece outerwear will keep you warm—wet or dry—and provides an excellent layer of insulation. For mountain afternoons, when the skies tend to open up and dump incredible amounts of water from the heavens, always carry a waterproof outer layer.

Being Prepared for the Unexpected

During a day of mountain angling, many things can go wrong. That's why I never go fishing without a day pack loaded with basic, lightweight survival gear. My pack is stuffed with a raincoat, rain pants, and an insulating layer to go beneath the shell. A couple of high-energy snacks are in the zipper pouch to give me a boost if I'm tired. For the unexpected trip through the dark, you'll find a flashlight with extra bulbs and batteries there, too. In case I'm out much longer than expected, I also carry matches and a container of fire starter. Even among former Boy Scouts, I know few woodsmen who can get a warm blaze going with wet wood. A multi-tool pocketknife is also in the pouch to help with a hundred things. Top it off with a first-aid kit, and I'm never out hiking with the feeling that I forgot something valuable. My completely loaded pack hangs on a hook in the garage, always ready for a spur-of-the-moment excursion.

Ticks

The mountains are indeed home to a variety of critters, but anglers have little to worry about from bears, mountain lions, and other large mammals. Perhaps the worst threat from the animal kingdom comes from ticks. These pinhead-to teardrop-sized creatures can carry two diseases—Rocky Mountain spotted fever and Lyme disease. Avoid both by always checking for ticks on your skin, particularly in your hair, in your armpits, and in your groin, after any trip along the stream. Ticks are most active before runoff subsides in July, so anglers can easily avoid them.

Wading Swift Waters

Only fly fishers wade, and the sport is closely identified with the sight of an angler standing midstream, awash in the liquid environment of a trout. I take my wading personally, and water washing over my feet, ankles, and calves is part of the purification process of angling.

There is, however, an inherent danger in wading mountain streams. Swift-moving water, polished rocks, and slimy coatings of algae conspire to make the foot-to-stream-bottom contact a tenuous meeting. Deep holes can occur on even small rivers. Tumbling down a rocky stream can lead to broken limbs or worse. With cold and hypothermia always lurking just over the mountain peaks, taking a dunking can have serious repercussions.

Swift water is obviously a hazard when wading, but places with water-worn, rounded gravel can also lead to an unexpected fall. Stream bottoms in granite mountains are slick, because they are loaded with tumbled rocks that offer no secure footing. Watch out also for sections of streams that have light layers of algae growing on the rocks. These slimy surfaces will have you doing a watery shuffle in no time at all. Turbid waters hold hidden dangers in the form of unseen cobbles and deep holes, so avoid wading when the water is muddy. It's a good idea to forgo wading when streams are running at full tilt, such as during spring runoff or following heavy downpours in the summer.

Wading often is overdone in mountain streams. With most of the streams small in size, there is rarely a need to wade in the water to reach the opposite bank with a cast. Just as rarely will you find it necessary to ease into the water to reduce the chance of being spied on the bank by a trout.

Always try casting from the bank first. If that doesn't produce the desired result, wade along the edge of the stream to avoid the forceful currents of water cascading over rocks. Like a trout, you can use the protection offered by instream boulders to reduce the force of the current.

If you must wade out into faster water, take slow, deliberate steps. The motion is like that of a skater—move one foot at a time, always placing one foot in front of or behind the other. You can easily be thrown off balance when you stand with your feet close together. Slide your foot along the bottom and try to feel the surface so that you can locate a solid placement. Avoid putting your weight on rounded rocks, and always ease your weight onto a rock to test how slick it is. When you have a solid foundation, move the other foot. Advancement or retreat is from 6 inches to a foot at a time. Face upstream, but angle across the stream or slightly downstream when moving your feet. When you are in position to make

High-altitude pocket water like this on Elk Creek in southern Colorado requires cautious wading.

your cast, check the security of your feet before you turn your attention to the trout.

It may be hard to resist, but don't overstep the limits of comfortable, safe wading. Turn back before you get into a situation where the current is tearing the gravel from beneath your feet. If you find yourself in this predicament, don't turn around. Instead, ease backward with your feet and feel the security of each step. Continue until the pull of the current is reduced and you feel comfortable.

If you do fall, don't panic, and don't attempt to swim upstream—thrashing about will only waste a lot of energy. Instead, swing your feet so that your legs are pointing downstream and ride the current. Bounce your feet off the bottom, or, if the stream is rocky, keep your feet up to push yourself off the rocks. As you float downstream, work your way to the bank as quickly as possible.

LIGHTNING

During July and August in the southern Rockies, you can almost set your watch by the timing of the first thunderclap of the day. And, as I'd hoped, the billowing cumulonimbus clouds shaded the deep runs of the Pine River and a nice little hatch of pale morning duns came off the water like snowflakes in reverse. More to the point, the resident browns were taking the mayflies, frequently mistaking my little Cahill for the real thing. Engrossed in the angling, I ignored the approaching storm, even as a light rain hissed on the water. As long as the trout rose, I wasn't about to stop fishing. What's a gallon of rain down the collar when the hatch is on? Besides, down in the canyon bottom, I had no fear of the flashes of lightning that danced from the clouds a mile overhead.

That is, until the river lit up like a gigantic flashbulb. Before I could react, a snap was followed by an explosion that seemed to burst inside my chest. Two hundred feet downstream, splinters from a solitary Douglas fir—the target for a spear of electrons thrown from the clouds—were tossed into the water like matchsticks. In two seconds, I was out of the water and into a nearby grove of trees. When my heart stopped drumming, I resolved not to be so cavalier about lightning.

Lightning is brewed from tropical moisture and warm, rising air. Heat the ground with intense summer sun, and air naturally rises, particularly along mountains and coastlines where cool temperatures are just a double-haul cast away. The ingredients boil into tall thunderheads, a familiar sight throughout the southern half of North America.

The mechanism of lightning formation is still much in debate, but the basic process goes something like this. Water droplets are carried along with the rising air, and once they get high enough, they partially freeze. Moving so rapidly skyward tears off some of the electrons on the ice particles, creating a positive charge in the rising air and leaving the bottom of the cloud with a negative charge. As the cloud base passes over the earth, it induces a positive charge on the surface directly below, setting up a huge capacitor. When the difference in charge is great enough, electrons from the cloud travel a narrow path toward the ground. Tall objects on the ground shorten the distance to the cloud and become the sites of lightning strikes.

A single bolt is worthy of deep respect. The electric discharge travels at 60,000 miles per hour over distances as great as 2 miles. The energy in a lightning flash could light a 100-watt light bulb for more than three months. The air near a lightning strike is heated instantly to 50,000 degrees Fahrenheit—hotter than the surface of the sun. This is what causes the familiar cracking sound called thunder.

More than 40 million lightning bolts zap the United States each year, resulting in about 100 deaths. The most lightning-caused deaths occur in Florida, with the Rocky Mountain region running a close second. The grim statistics are packed with golfers, hikers, boaters, and anglers who ignored or were unaware of the danger posed by lightning.

While the presence of thunderstorms calls for caution, there is no need to cower in fear all summer long. A few simple rules will help keep you from danger when a storm is nearby.

Although the chances of taking a direct hit from lightning are slim, an angler standing on open ground along a lake or in a river, holding a graphite electrical conductor in his or her hands, unwittingly increases the likelihood of taking a strike. The most basic rule of lightning safety is to seek shelter. If possible, head straight for your car, which is the best place to ride out the storm. It's not the rubber tires that protect you—the metal car body channels the currents to the ground around the passengers inside.

When should you run from the storm? Much of the danger from cloud-to-ground electric discharge lies in the fact that outdoor enthusiasts seldom seek shelter from a storm until they start to get wet. In fact, most lightning-caused deaths occur at the beginning or end of a storm when no rain is falling. Lightning can strike more than 5 miles away from the generating thunderstorm, with no advance warning. So, if you employ the time-honored "flash-and-boom" countdown method—the storm is a mile away from every five seconds of delay between lightning and thunder—don't assume you are safe because you know the storm is miles away. The reality is, if you can hear thunder, you are close enough to be struck by lightning. Head for shelter immediately.

Few anglers are aware that you don't have to actually get hit by lightning to be severely injured by it. A lightning strike sets up a current that passes through the ground. This is often as deadly as the main jolt and covers a much larger area.

In order to correct the electric imbalance created at the point of the strike, electrons flood to the spot from a radius as much as 100 feet away. This ground current creates a deadly flow of electricity within the circle. Ground currents are a hazard near trees, rocks, or other tall objects that may be targets for lightning.

Avoid anything that increases your electrical connection with the ground. Golfers in spikes are a well-known example, but what about anglers wading in a stream? Anglers are well connected with the ground through the water, which, of course, is a good conductor of electrical current. To be on the safe side, always leave the stream during a storm just to avoid being so well connected to the ground through the water.

A graphite rod is a good lightning rod. Fiberglass rods also conduct electricity when they are wet. Wet fly line is also a fair conductor and can carry current when lightning strikes near the water.

It's not unheard of for a fly fisher to get totally wrapped up in the business at hand. When a storm sneaks up on you and there's no chance of reaching the safety of your car, keep a level head. Stay on low ground and look for a wooded area. Good protection can be found in groups of same-sized trees. In open areas, avoid lone trees or rocks. Stay out of depressions, shallow caves, and overhangs, where ground currents might jump across the openings and endanger you.

When you are out in the open, you know you're in real trouble if you catch a whiff of the pungent odor of ozone, if your skin tingles, or if the hair on your arms and neck stands on end. Throw your rod as far away as you can. Crouch down (don't lie flat), place your feet close together, put your hands on your knees, and place your head between your knees. In this awkward position, you'll be a low, small target, and it will minimize the chance of ground currents using your body as a path for electrons.

A lightning-strike victim needs immediate help. No residual electrical charge is present, and the person can be handled safely. Even victims who appear dead often can be revived with prompt action. If possible, send for emergency medical help. The American Red Cross recommends mouth-to-mouth resuscitation for strike victims who are not breathing. If both pulse and breathing are absent, cardiopulmonary resuscitation is required. This procedure should be attempted only by persons who are properly trained.

Even victims who appear to be only stunned need attention. Send for medical assistance, keep the victims warm, and have them rest. Check for burns, especially at fingers and toes and next to buckles and jewelry.

It's tough to walk away from the river when the hatch is on and the fish are cooperative, but when lightning cuts through the clouds above, packing up is the only way to ensure the opportunity to fish the next day. Keep an eye on the sky, seek shelter well before the storm arrives, and enjoy the light show.

Chapter Two

Packing It In

I'm familiar with most of the small streams in northern New Mexico, so when the well-respected outdoor writer Dave Hughes came to town looking for an out-of-the-way place to wet a fly, he asked me to take him to a favorite spot. As we stretched our legs after the rough drive over poor excuses for roads, Dave opened the back of his truck and lifted the lid to a secret compartment, exposing more rod tubes than you find in most fly-fishing shops.

"You picked an 8½-foot, 5 weight for this water," he said as he gave my rod the once-over. "Would you recommend I do the same?"

I nodded in agreement, knowing my embarrassment would show if I spoke. I hadn't selected the rod especially for the water we were to fish. It was the only rod I owned. I didn't want to appear to be a rank amateur, so I did my best to hide what I suddenly perceived was a serious flaw in my fly-fishing arsenal.

If my writing talent and book sales matched those of John Grisham, it might be a different situation. But as it is, I live on a limited budget, and, although it remains my number-one outdoor passion, I have far too many interests in life to sink a lot of money into fly fishing. There are mountain bikes, backpacking stoves, computer peripherals, and saxophones out there calling my name. Plus, the kids keep wearing out their shoes and growing out of their jeans every few months. So, to stay within the limits of my restricted discretionary income, I'm forced to make choices about what to buy, and unless you're a corporate executive, childless, and single, I suspect you live the same way.

I've fished many hours since that day when I felt insecure about owning only one rod, but I've never bought another. I confess that I now own two rods, but the second one was a gift. I've never regretted sinking a princely sum into that fine, 8½-foot, 5-weight rod. It cost about twice what I intended to pay, but when I figure how many hours it has spent touching my palms, it's been a sound investment.

Mountain water is as diverse as the fine pale ales brewed on the West Coast, and the angling authorities who get their thoughts set in 10-point type will tell you that it takes a different rod to fish each type of water. For nymphing on a wide-open, main river, a 9½-foot, 6- or 7-weight rod is ideal to chuck hunks of lead to the far bank. The same rod will get you into a nightmare of tangles on a brush-lined, closed-in canyon stream filled with wild trout; only a 7-foot, 4-weight rod will do in such close quarters. For delicate presentations on a window-sheen surface of a meadow meander, a 2-weight rod 8 feet in length is perfect. Throwing nymphs on lakes requires a 9-foot, 6-weight rod.

The experts are absolutely right—there is an ideal rod for every situation in fly fishing. Does that mean you have to spend a fortune on a half-dozen rods to catch trout? I don't believe so. You have to admit to yourself that what the experts say is true, then go out and buy yourself a compromise—a rod that will be *nearly* the perfect one in a variety of situations.

The best mountain water often lies far from the road and requires an overnight stay in the backcountry.

You may be surprised to discover that the one rod you need to fish mountain water is the one you already have. Most of us start our fly-fishing career with a compromise rod of medium to long length and modest weight, say 8½ feet long designed for a 5-weight line. Such a rod will get you through all but the extreme conditions on mountain water. You might regret having such a rod when chucking streamers to pockets in front of blocks of rock in a big river on a windy day, but chances are you wouldn't have a great time with any *other* rod in that situation. The brush along a headwater trickle can cause you to wish for a 6-footer, but you can compensate by using some clever techniques, and they won't cost you a penny.

Although I believe you don't need to spend a lot of money for a closet full of rods, I heartily recommend that you be prepared to sink a sizable investment into the one compromise rod that you do buy. Think of how many hours each summer that rod will spend in your hand. You want a rod that is comfortable and easy to use. Because most of your casting will be flipping, you don't want a stiff rod, but because you need to be fairly accurate, you don't want a stick that will flap in the breeze either. Moderation is the key. A well-built, medium-action rod is well worth the extra money. Look for an 8- to 8½-foot, 4- to 6-weight rod made of graphite in the $350 to $450 range. It's an investment you won't regret.

There is one important rod-selection decision to make, however. Because an invigorating hike is often a prelude to mountain-water fishing, you need to look closely at the choice between two-piece, three-piece, and four-piece rods. In the not-too-distant past, the action and response of four-piece fly rods were noticeably inferior to those of standard rods, and most anglers went with the superior two-section sticks. In the last decade, rod-building techniques and materials have changed, and there is virtually no difference between the feel of well-built rods with any number of sections.

It's hard to resist nice-looking trailside pools, so on an overnight trip, consider carrying your rod on the hike into camp.

The obvious advantage of a four-piece rod is its short breakdown length, which is usually between 20 and 24 inches. It is convenient to throw in a backpack, allowing your hands to be free during the hike to the water. For air travel, you can throw the rod tube into your carry-on luggage and rest easy, knowing your rod will reach your destination along with you, not hidden in a crack in a 727's cargo hold. For a mountain-bike fishing excursion, a four-piece rod is essential, for although you can strap a long rod tube to your handlebars and pedal off, there isn't, to my knowledge, a safe way to transport a two-piece rod on a bike.

On short hikes to a fishing hole, carrying a long rod presents no problems. Two-piece or four-piece, it matters not. It's nice to have your hands free on a longer hike, and a four-piece rod on your back is well suited for such adventures. But consider this: If the hike is leading you upstream, you'll probably be tempted to test the water every time you walk near a hole that is too good to pass by. I wind up carrying a fully rigged rod on most hikes, even on backpacking trips, and stop frequently to "bio-sample" and find out what kind of trout live in every reach of stream. This technique makes for a more pleasant, albeit slow, hike to a destination and makes a moot point out of carrying a rod that fits easily into my backpack.

Weigh your needs carefully before you decide to get a travel rod, which is usually more expensive than its two-piece counterpart. You'll find slightly more versatility in a four-piece rod, but with the two rod types so similar, it might not be worth the added expense.

Let's Get Reel

I just took a long, hard look at my favorite fly reel, and it's not a pretty sight. The rim has more nicks than a motorcycle windshield on a New Mexico highway, and two former dents bear the imprint of the teeth of the pliers that were needed to bend them back into proper shape. The reel's back face looks like it's been scratched by a bobcat, and the manufacturer's logo is worn and completely unreadable.

You see, my reel has accompanied me on many falls and has often taken the full force of a blow against sharp rocks. It's part of the nature of mountain fishing—you spend a lot of time moving on slippery rocks, in or out of the water. Odds are, you won't always remain upright. If you can think fast enough on your brief journey to the ground, your first instinct is to protect your rod. When you raise the fragile rod tip, the butt of the rod usually stays down, and on a hard fall, it is the reel that more often than not gets whacked.

Taking a finely crafted, expensive fly reel into the backcountry is like driving a Porsche on a dirt road to the trailhead. It's just asking for costly trouble. You wouldn't want your sports car to get banged on rocks or dunked in a stream; treat your best reel with the same respect.

A simple-action, small- to medium-size, inexpensive fly reel is well suited for mountain water, and you won't feel bad when it gets banged around. You'll rarely have more than 20 feet of line off the reel anyway, and most stream trout won't rip off yards of line during even the toughest fight; they're more likely to just try and break you off against the rocks.

My old reel looks like hell, but it still sings a sweet tune. One simple piece of advice: Once you are off the water, take good care of your mountain-water reel. Always dry it out at the end of the day and keep it well lubricated.

LINES AND LEADERS

Call me old-fashioned, but I find brightly colored fly lines distracting. Splitting a jewel-like mountain pool in half with an fluorescent orange fly line seems profane. Mountain-water anglers would do well to stick with pale, subtle-colored fly lines. Look for one in pale green, faded orange, or ivory.

With the short distances and small flies involved, it's tempting to think that you can get away with a light, 2-weight outfit for mountain water. Because most of your casting will be done with flips, however, it's important to have as much mass as you can in the fly line. Anything less than 4-weight just doesn't seem to carry the momentum of a flip cast, making it difficult to be as accurate as you'd like to be. A heavier line also gives more control when you are using the long-arm technique for fishing complex currents in pocket water or on rocky freestone streams, and quick mends are more sure when done with greater weight. For the same reasons, a weight-forward line will be to your advantage when you are tossing flies in tight quarters.

Once again, the middle of the road is the best course, and a 4- or 5-weight line matches the water, the flies, and the distances. For the same reason—to carry the momentum of a flip cast—look for weight-forward fly lines for all situations in the mountains. It will give you more distance for the punch.

I know a lot of anglers who relentlessly fuss over their leader and tippet. On the other hand, I think I've probably gone a whole summer without changing my leader. The fly line–leader connection has always driven me nuts, so I avoid dealing with it until I'm left with no choice. Given a 5X, 8- or 9-foot leader, I can adjust the total length of my fly connection by varying the tippet length. Because you hardly ever need more than 8 or 9 feet between your fly line and fly, and because a 5X tippet will see you through almost all mountain-water situations, this system is easy to manage and saves my sanity by making me deal with nail knots only a few times a year. There are situations that call for special leaders and tippets, but they are rare.

Wading in Deeper

Chest waders are usually overkill when you are fishing mountain water. They're hot, and you'll drown in your own sweat if you wear them to hike into a stream. Even light-weight ones are much too bulky to permit the freedom of movement that you need to boulder-hop along headwaters.

When the situation calls for waders—such as when the water is frigid snowmelt or when you are trying to keep dry on a chilly, overcast morning—stocking-foot hippers are the key. With an old pair of hiking boots and gravel guards, you can comfortably hike to your destination in your waders and have solid footing on the way. I've gotten many years out of the pair of neoprene hippers that seem to have fallen out of fashion, but they are unbeatable for warmth and agility and they cling to my legs better than the newer, more lightweight materials. Hip waders have the advantage of being rather light and small of bulk, giving you the option of stuffing them in a day pack and carrying them to your destination.

Over the years, I've found that summer and early fall fishing can be done without the benefit of waders. Wet wading offers high mobility, the most comfort, and a carefree style of movement. The market now offers a wide variety of quick-drying, synthetic materials that come in shorts or long pants. With them you can splash around all morning and be dry by the end of lunch.

For footwear you have two practical options. Wearing an old pair of hiking boots makes it possible to bring only one pair of shoes for both the hike into the water and the wading. A pair of fleece socks can add comfort when it's a bit chilly. One caution: When you wear wet boots, watch for rubbing and blisters on the hike out.

I'm sold on all-terrain sandals for wet wading. Originally designed by river runners, this lightweight, airy footwear was built for water first and hiking second. The combination is almost perfect for mountain water. Wear your amphibious footwear to the stream, in the stream, and comfortably back to camp. However, sandals aren't slip-proof, and they offer no ankle support or protection for your toes from rocks. Look for a pair of all-terrain sandals with heavy straps that will secure the sandals tightly to your feet and with soles that offer solid footing on submerged rocks. Wade sockless or with fleece or neoprene socks, and carry an extra pair in your pack for warm feet on the way back to camp.

Packing It In

When your favorite hole is three miles from the road, how do you get all your fly-fishing paraphernalia there? And when you're hitting forty miles of trail to cover a variety of water, how do you pare down the load?

For a short jaunt in from the road—let's say less than 2 miles—grab your vest and head out. Stuff a sandwich, a small water bottle, and a raincoat in the otherwise worthless vest back pocket and you're set for a couple hours of fun.

But when you plan to spend some part of your day hiking into the stream or lake, the volume of gear increases to the point where a vest isn't very comfortable. It's time for a good day pack—one that will hold a day's worth of food, water, clothing, flies, and assorted gear. Everything you need for a day can fit into a modest-sized day pack with a couple of straps on the outside to lash on a raincoat or a pair of sandals. If you want to spend the bucks, a few manufacturers have created ingenious front/back pack combinations that offer accessibility and volume.

For serious fishing day trips, you may want to stuff your pack with your vest and perhaps a pair of waders. When you're headed on such a journey, consider a small-volume, internal-frame, "overnighter" pack. Comfortable and roomy, internal frames can carry all your gear and give you many options to adjust the load for maximum comfort and flexibility. These packs are large enough to carry raincoats, warm clothing, waders, lunch, and every fly box you own. When you get the adjustments right, you can wear the pack all day, even when fishing, and not notice any loss of mobility.

For backpacking trips to distant waters, you'll want to pare down all you can from your gear. Instead of a vest, try a fisherman's lanyard, a simple necklace that permits you to clip on your essential tools—clippers, hemostats, fly grease, and a spool of tippet. Like a vest, the lanyard keeps everything within easy reach but does so with very little bulk or weight.

Buy a couple of small fly boxes and stuff them with an assortment of backcountry flies—attractors, terrestrials, a few lake patterns, and caddis. If you wear shirts or pants that have large cargo pockets, you can carry the fly boxes there; otherwise, a small hip pack can keep your flies easily accessible.

When fishing hike-in water, travel light, using a lanyard and pants with plenty of pockets instead of a vest.

When you head into the backcountry, always split your flies into at least two boxes, just in case one floats away or otherwise gets lost.

I hate to mention it, but your rod *can* break in the backcountry. On your hike into mountain water, you're likely to be walking through overhanging trees, snarling weeds, and trailside rocks—each a potential rod-snapper. Without a protective case, the safest way to transport your rod on a trail is to break it down into two sections. The shorter length helps keep the tip out of overhanging branches. It's also a good idea to walk with the rod pointing behind you. This prevents jamming a tip into a tree trunk or a rock.

You're finally at the wilderness lake of your dreams, twenty miles into the backcountry. Salivating, you pull your rod from its case and snap—broken tip. It's so sad to see a grown fly fisher cry. Don't suffer this cruel lesson. For long, overnight trips, always take a spare rod.

Mountain Bikes, Horses, and Llamas

Although mountain fishing seems synonymous with hiking, there's more than one way to reach remote fishing spots. Instead of walking, you can ride a bike. The fat tires and low gear ratios of mountain bikes permit you to pedal up reasonably steep forest roads and trails, over rocks, and around minor obstacles. A mountain bike can be a poor man's four-wheel drive, with one important advantage—you can always carry your bike over severe obstacles and stay out of trouble that way. For mountain-water anglers, a bike can provide a means to get to remote fishing holes quickly.

There is a price to pay, of course. Don't expect a mountain bike to do much for you if you aren't in reasonably good physical condition. Hauling yourself and 28 pounds of bicycle up a steep, rocky trail requires some degree of technical riding ability, but it definitely requires strength and endurance. Don't expect to buy a bike and hit the trail to some high-country lake the next day. It takes time to develop your legs to the point where they can ungrudgingly take you into the backcountry.

Compared to hiking, a mountain bike will allow you to cover extensive chunks of ground in a day, giving you more time on the water instead of on the trail. Intermediate bike riders can easily cover 12 to 15 or even 20 miles in a day. Such a range leaves walking anglers behind and opens up a whole new set of places to fish where the other guy ain't.

Here in the southern Rockies, the best use of a mountain bike for fly fishing comes in the very early season, either pre-runoff on the larger streams or early post-runoff on the headwaters. From late March to mid-May, many of the forest-access roads to fishing are gated shut, closed to vehicles but still open to hikers and bikers. Short patches of snow still block the roads, keeping out 99 out of 100 anglers. It doesn't take much effort to push a bike over or around a snowbank, and that leaves me with a treasure chest of streams that haven't seen an angler for five months. Most of the locations are just a few miles in from the highway, so in half an hour, I'm on the water.

You can take a bike to a remote lake or headwater stream, or you can fish midsections of long streams with easy access at the ends. One good example is Hermosa Creek, a few miles north of Durango, Colorado. Forest roads lead to the upper and lower stretches of stream, but the 10 miles between are accessible only by trail. With a mountain bike, you can ride past 99 percent of the anglers on the water. In less than half an hour of pedaling, you can have 4 miles of Hermosa Creek to yourself—reason enough to buy a bike.

Mountain bikes are not welcome on every mile of trail in the mountains, and they are prohibited on all trails in wilderness areas. In general, any road open to vehicles is legal for

When traveling by mountain bike, the only safe way to carry a fly rod is in its case in a backpack.

bikes, and that opens up a lot of lakes at the end of jeep roads that most folks don't get to. Be a responsible rider and always yield a trail to hikers and horseback riders.

One problem remains: How do you transport your rod while you are riding a mountain bike? Here's one case where a four-piece rod gives you a decided advantage. Strapping a four-piece rod in a protective tube to a backpack is the best, safest way—for rider and rod—to combine biking and angling. It is possible to carry a two-piece rod on a bike, either lashed to a pack or to the handlebars, but either method leaves much to be desired. A long rod on your back is not only awkward, it has a propensity to bang constantly into your bike helmet. On a trail, it frequently catches on tree branches, bringing you to an unexpected, often painful stop. Strapping your rod in its protective tube to the handlebars is a better method of transport, but on narrow trails, it requires some skillful bike handling to keep the added width of the tube from scraping the trees. I recommend trail riding with four-piece rods only.

If providing your own power to reach a distant lake or headwater stream sounds too extreme, you can use the time-honored method of horsepacking. Trading tired legs for a sore butt is actually a fine way to get into remote mountain lakes that might require several days of uncomfortable back-packing to reach. Most horse trips involve a drop-off and pick-up several days later, so once you reach your destination, you don't have to worry about livestock.

Backcountry outfitters are found in most mountain towns. Because horses have potential negative impacts on trails and sensitive backcountry areas, you want to find an outfitter who has a sense of environmental caring. You can usually get an idea of sensitivity from the outfitter's brochure or web site.

Llamas are acquiring a strong presence in the mountain wilderness areas of the West. The gentle, easy-to-manage beasts of burden are well suited to carrying heavy loads—usually up to 70 pounds—far into the backcountry. You still have to walk, but leading a llama up a steep trail is much eas-ier than carrying a monster pack. Llamas carry less than horses but are usually less expensive.

Llama tours can be guided drop-offs, or you can rent a llama, usually after receiving a brief training course on llama care. Care for llamas in the wilderness is usually easy, but such a trip is not as carefree as a simple drop-off. Unlike horses, llamas can follow just about any trail a human can, so the potential for adventure and great angling is far better with llamas than with horses.

Chapter Three

Match the Water, Not the Hatch

Late September in Colorado's San Juan Mountains is capped by a sky so intense that it is almost purple. Groves of aspen glow on the mountainsides, and there's a nip to the morning air, reminding you that the edge of winter is only a month away, if that. On this particular day, summer lingered over the mountains like a lover reluctant to part from his sweetheart. Our coffee water froze solid during the night, but by midmorning it was warm enough for us to work up a good sweat as we hiked 3 miles in along the Piedra River. My fishing partner, Don, and I thrashed the water with hundreds of casts. Don took a heavy brown off a submerged white sandstone ledge with a Royal Wulff, but I came up empty. We stopped for lunch, offering each other a swarm of worthless explanations on why the fish were lethargic.

Back on the water under the afternoon sun, a couple of small mayflies hovered above a riffle. I tied on a size 16 Ginger Dun Parachute, a wisp of a fly that I often resort to using when confronted with finicky feeders. I popped the pattern into a swirl of current beneath the shade of an alder and watched it bob with the bubbles churned up by a nearby rock. In a moment, the fly was pulled from view by what proved to be a rainbow that sucked it deep into his mouth. I quickly returned the fish to the water, dried the fly on my shirttail, and spun off another cast to a pocket just upstream. The result was another nice rainbow.

"Solved it!" I shouted upstream to Don as the rainbow kicked its tail and dissolved back into the rocks. As I moved to tell him that small, reddish flies were the answer, I noticed that he, too, was releasing a fish.

"Got it!" he shouted back. "Yellow grasshoppers—size 6."

We both found the answer to fooling trout on that afternoon, only there were two answers and they were as different as night and day. Chunky hoppers or delicate mayflies were the key. We stuck to our chosen patterns, taking fish regularly for the next half hour. Curious, I changed to a Parachute Hopper and continued my stretch of luck. Fish kept hitting when I switched from the hopper to the House and Lot, then to a Brown Wulff.

Clearly, on that afternoon, pattern selection was unimportant. As is most often the case in mountain water, the trout didn't care what they were eating. I suspect that while we ate lunch and argued about trout, the noon sun had finally warmed the water, chilled by the previous night's frost, to the threshold for trout feeding. Don and I didn't "solve the problem," we just took advantage of a change in the behavior of the trout. As long as our flies floated true on the currents, trout would take them.

Opportunity Knocks

As one trained in biology, I have always been most intrigued by matching the hatch. The sense of sport given by fooling trout with handcrafted imitations of their natural food is at the core of fly fishing. When I started out, I picked up most of the basics of the sport from books and videos, and every one of them taught the gospel of fishing the natural insect. For many years I believed I could increase my chances with every trout if I fished the perfect pattern. The necessity of matching the hatch turned out to be one of the great myths of fly fishing.

The truth is, on mountain waters you rarely come across an instance where you must match the natural insect. In my experience, mountain fish feed selectively on a single insect only 5 to 10 percent of the time. So no matter how logical—no matter how proper it seems to give the fish exactly what they are used to seeing—all that preaching about matching the hatch doesn't make a bit of difference in the real world of mountain streams. But that doesn't mean you'll catch a fish every time you present a fly.

In mountain streams, brook trout, cutthroats, and even rainbows often lash at the same fly on successive casts. I have a tongue-in-cheek rule—two looks at the same fly means the fish is probably a rainbow; three looks, a cutthroat; and four or more, the fish has to be a brook trout. Brown trout will give you only one chance. (I'm not so naive to believe this is true, but it makes for some fun on the water. After all, fly fishing is a sport, not a religion.) It's not uncommon to have a fish strike, shake off the hook, then come right back on the next cast and take the fly with confidence a second time. Fair-sized brookies will even chase a fish on the end of a line in a comical effort to snatch the fly from the mouth of their hooked brethren.

This willingness to strike at anything has given backcountry trout, particularly brookies and cutthroats, a reputation for being just plain stupid. But as a host of wise writers have said before me, these fish are simply following well-developed survival instincts. In a world that presents few opportunities for feeding, these trout are taking advantage of every reasonable chance to grab some nourishment.

Blame the mountain trout's willingness to feed on its habitat. Aside from clean, well-aerated water, high-country streams have little to offer trout. The foundation of a stream's food chain is decaying plant material. The short mountain growing season limits the amount of nutrient from plants entering the system. A second limit is imposed by the constricted size of the watersheds and their component streams. Not much base nutrient is added to the system each year. One step up the food chain, the insects that feed on plant material are scarce. In addition, the active season for insects, the main components of the trout's diet, is relatively short. In mountain water, there isn't much on the menu, and the restaurant is always about to close.

The energy dynamics of mountain streams play to the advantage of anglers. While the summer sun shines, trout must eat. As a result, mountain trout are rarely selective feeders. Instead, they are willing and frequent risers. In order to obtain the food energy that they need to survive, trout take repeated chances. They inspect by sight or taste almost everything that happens by.

Most of the time and in most places, your choice of fly pattern is no more important than the color of your jockey shorts. When conditions are right, and they often are on mountains streams, trout will grab aggressively at anything that vaguely resembles a food item. This applies not only to the young and inexperienced fish, but to the king of each hole.

I've seen this proven time and again by the Ugly Humpy. Tying flies is not one of my most impressive skills, and hair-bodied patterns are a particular weakness. My Humpys are sloppy, and the materials are not always securely tied to the hook. In my case, Goofus Bug is by far the more appropriate name. After hooking a couple of trout, especially brookies with their razor-sharp teeth, my Humpy's body is frayed and its hackle is often turned into a trailing wing. The result looks like a teenage mutant butterfly, certainly nothing like any real insect I've ever come across.

But when the fish are hitting, I'm too impatient to cut off a bedraggled Humpy and tie on a prettier fly. The thing is, more often than not, the Ugly Humpy continues to take good fish. Have I stumbled on the perfect imitation of some rare stream insect? Probably not. The explanation is simply that opportunistic feeders zero in on the floating motion of anything that is buglike on the currents.

What I'm telling you is that not every stream is a spring creek, and 90 out of 100 fish are not educated. I think that fly fishers perpetuate stories about the necessity of outwitting fish with the perfect pattern to make it easier to explain it away when they get skunked. (It works for me.) In the real world of mountain water, just about anything that rides on the currents will get at least a look from a trout, including beat-up fly patterns, strike indicators, twigs, and leaves.

The characteristic of mountain trout to strike at anything has been observed as far back as the beginning of the written record of North American history. In his *Memorial of 1630*, Fray Alonso Benavides reported from New Mexico to his superiors in Spain the exploits of a detachment of soldiers exploring the foothills of the Sangre de Cristo Mountains. Benavides picked up the soldiers' tale on the Gallinas River outside present day Las Vegas, New Mexico.

> They traveled until they came to a beautiful stream along whose banks grew many plum trees. The waters were filled with trout. In less than three hours, with bare hooks, the men were able to catch 40 arrobas weight.

If you lack the skill to convert from arrobas to pounds, the soldiers caught about one thousand pounds of native cutthroat.

Incidentally, this is probably the first written record of angling in North America with an artificial lure—if you permit an unbaited hook to be so classified.

Let's dispense with this "you've-got-to-have-the-perfect-fly" thing. Pattern selection on mountain water is relatively unimportant. Impressionistic or realistic, it matters not. Forget about the pattern and concentrate on reading the water and on your presentation.

In the absence of any guidance from the trout, how do you select a fly pattern to use on mountain water? If the fish don't seem to care what pattern you use, why not pick flies that give you an advantage? For mountain water angling, match the water, not the hatch.

Mountain streams hand me the luxury of fishing with the patterns in which I have the most confidence. Over the years, I've come to trust the patterns that float well on swift currents and that I can see well on the water. Certain styles of flies are designed for specific water types—broken currents, pockets, runs, or riffles. You can choose a fly that you can see well in the type of water you are exploring and one that rides high and dry, even after taking a dive.

And seeing is just the point. Confidence comes when you can see the fly well enough on the water in order to set the hook when a trout hits it. You rarely see trout rising on mountain-water streams because the currents carry away rise forms in a moment. You must know where the fly is so that you can see the strike. It helps to have a fly with a light wing or post that will remain visible on every cast under a variety of light conditions.

The fly must also be appropriate for the current conditions. For example, both a House and Lot and a Parachute Adams have white wings, but they are best used in different types of water. In fast, foamy currents, the bushy House and Lot stays afloat and is easy for the angler—and the trout—to see. But on choppy runs or smooth stretches of stream, the

High-floating, high-visibility flies with bushy wings are required for mountain-water fishing.

House and Lot sometimes falls short. The Parachute Adams sits lightly on the water, presenting a sparse silhouette to the fish. It's perfect for less turbulent runs.

In pocket water and on roaring freestone streams, you must have flies that can take a dunking and still come up to the surface. Fly patterns that work well in foaming water have a jungle of hackle, puffy bodies, or bushy wings. Delicate hackle-fiber tails, hackle-tip wings, or quill feathers are discarded for more buoyant, durable materials like calf tail, elk body hair, or deer fur.

The simplest high-floating flies are of the Wulff series. They derive their high flotation from heavy hackling and the use of hair for wings and tails. Extremely versatile, Wulff flies can be tied in gray, white, brown, yellow (known as the Grizzly Wulff), or royal. Each style uses a moose- or deer-hair tail; squirrel, elk, or calf wings; and perhaps a dozen turns of suitable hackle. Of the heavy-water flies I use, the Wulffs are the easiest to tie.

Fore-and-aft hackled flies like the Renegade are another simple pattern for fast-moving water. The double hackle provides high-floating properties on a delicate fly. The profusion of hackle strikes me as a good imitation of moving wings, particularly in low light. With a peacock body and brown hackle in the rear and white in front, the Renegade is easy to spot, even in low light conditions. For that reason, I use it or its relatives (like the Warden's Worry, which substitutes grizzly for the white hackle) most often as the sun drops behind canyon walls.

Hair bodies of deer or elk fibers produce more flotation than other styles of flies. Each fiber of these furs is hollow and traps air inside, making the flies very floatable. The Humpy is the most popular of the hair-bodied flies, and with good reason. It floats well all day in the roughest water and imitates a wide variety of insects, from caddis flies to grasshoppers. The basic color of the fly can be varied with the use of different-colored threads for the underbody, with yellow, red, orange, or green the most effective. The overbody is a simple layer of deer hair forming a hump on the back. When in doubt while fishing choppy water, I often try a Humpy first.

High-floating flies with clipped hair bodies are the most buoyant, water-resistant patterns. Deer hair can be difficult to work with, and beginning fly tiers might want to start by using caribou for clipped hair bodies. Caribou is easy to spin on a hook and trims up well. You might lose a bit of flotation and durability, but it's worth it to reduce stress.

With a stout body of trimmed deer fur, the classic Irresistible floats like Styrofoam, yet the natural color and texture of the materials make it surprisingly realistic. The traditional

BASIC MOUNTAIN-WATER FLIES AND WATER TYPES

Flies	Riffles	Slicks	Pools	Pocket Water	Meadow Water	Alpine Lake
Parachute Adams		X	X		X	X
Ginger Dun Parachute		X	X		X	
House and Lot	X			X		
Royal Humpy	X	X		X		
Goddard Caddis	X	X		X		
Elk Hair Caddis		X	X			
Irresistible	X			X		
Renegade	X			X	X	X
Stimulator	X	X		X		
Parachute Blue-Winged Olive			X		X	X
Parachute Brown Wulff	X	X		X	X	
Dave's Hopper		X			X	
Parachute Ant		X	X		X	
Foam Beetle						X
Dry Muddler	X	X		X	X	X
Olive Flymph						X
Partridge and Gray Soft Hackle						X
Black Woolly Bugger			X			X

Irresistible is tied with deer-hair wings and blue dun hackle, but the Adams Irresistible, with grizzly hackle-tip wings and hackle, is more suited for western waters.

A high-floating caddis pattern to use in broken water is the Goddard Caddis. It has a simple, clipped hair body trimmed to the triangular caddis shape, with a couple of hackles in front for more buoyancy. The gray deer-hair body can be colored with marking pens to match the wings of naturals.

Even before the optometrist told me that everyone needs glasses after they hit the age of forty, I started tying many fly patterns with upright white wings to increase my chances of picking them out on the water. Being all thumbs at the tying bench, I found the kinky hairs of a calf tail difficult to work with. I made life easier by substituting the more pliable white calf-body hair in my patterns.

I've taken my preference of white to an extreme. Instead of a traditional deer-hair wing on a Humpy, I use the royal version developed by Charles Ridenour. I put clipped white posts on my small Blue-Winged Olives. Tired of losing sight of black ant patterns on every cast, I started tying them parachute style with a white wing. You'll find white wings on my Irresistibles and Parachute Adams, too.

Another of my favorite high-country flies is the House and Lot, affectionately referred to as the H and L. I've never found anyone who could tell me the derivation of the name, but everyone who knows the fly has the feeling it has something to do with the way trout take it—wholeheartedly, like they were buying the complete package, home and yard. Just as consistently, most fly fishers can tell you this was President Dwight Eisenhower's favorite fly. Ike loved this fly for the same reason the rest of us do. He could always spot it on the water.

The beauty of the H and L is its white calf-tail wings and tail. The kinky hairs, combined with a thick skirt of brown hackle, keep the fly afloat high on the surface. The flashes of white both fore and aft bring the fly quickly into focus, whether it floats or takes a dunking. I believe the white wing shimmers as speckles of light reach a stream through the overhanging trees. The peculiar magic that peacock bodies work on trout adds to the fly's qualities, and thick brown hackle helps keep the fly riding high. You can fish the H and L in a size 10, and the fish don't seem to notice the preposterous size. It may be the perfect fly for mountain water.

So far I've painted a rather optimistic picture of catching trout on any old fly. Of course, it doesn't always work that way.

There are plenty of trout that would make a liar out of me if I tried to tell you they won't refuse a gaudy pattern. Trout living close to a road are more likely to refuse attractor flies, not because they are selective feeders, but because they've seen and been stung by fly patterns before. When the Humpy just doesn't make it, you can turn to something less garish.

Parachute flies are an excellent merger of floating ability, visibility, and the need for a more realistic silhouette. Parachute patterns are tied with the hackle wound parallel to the hook shank rather than perpendicular to it. They are designed to catch a lot of air during the cast, permitting the fly to float gently to the surface for a delicate presentation. The second advantage of the style is that the fly rides lower on the water, supported by the circular fibers of the hackle. This offers a more realistic way to represent legs on a mayfly pattern.

Few anglers look at parachute flies tied with a stiff tail of moose-body hair, natural dubbing, and high-quality hackle as excellent floaters in rough water. These flies are not as resilient as deer-hair bodied flies, but the broad hackle base of parachute flies permits them to ride well in choppy currents. The parachute design allows for inclusion of a white calf-tail or light elk-hair postwing that makes these flies easy to spot in broken water—just the prescription for the mountains.

When mayflies are on the water and my high-floating Humpy or House and Lot gets constant refusals from trout that I know I should be catching, I first turn to a parachute pattern. I'm not going for a delicate presentation here, but rather for a good floating pattern that looks more like the real thing. I use parachute patterns the same way I use any attractor fly, probing the pockets or casting to risers. On numerous occasions they have saved the day.

Again, you don't need to create a complicated series of parachute patterns to match whatever naturals you might find. Four or five parachute patterns are usually sufficient to cover 90 percent of the trickier situations that arise on mountain waters. Royal Wulffs tied parachute style are perfect for in-between water that is not too rough and not too smooth. In modest currents, a Parachute Adams tied with a white post often brings approval from more difficult trout. Along with these two, brown, ginger, and yellow bodies will cover most situations.

The best all-around parachute pattern for mountain waters is a little-seen member of the Wulff series, the Brown Wulff. I can't remember where I first saw the pattern, but it struck me as a fine imitation of the majority of brownish, tan, and reddish-brown mayflies found in the faster waters of the Rockies. It is a simple fly with a brown hackle-fiber tail, a dubbed brown rabbit-fur body, and mixed grizzly and red-brown hackle. For the parachute version, I use a light elk-hair postwing to add visibility. This simple fly has tricked more slightly fussy backcountry trout than any other in my box.

On mountain water, you'll hit places where the trout will hit anything. But if you aren't catching fish with your first fly choice to match the water, the first thing to change isn't the pattern but the size of the fly. I usually start with a size 12 pattern. At different times, a larger or smaller hook size will bring success. On roiling streams in Colorado or Wyoming, you can often change to a size 10 and start finding fish. It's hard for a mountain trout to resist such a hefty chunk of meat. If bigger doesn't lead to better, then drop down to size 14, but rarely to size 16.

If changing size doesn't change your success rate, then tie on the same pattern in a different color. Humpys usually come in yellow, but the red, green, or orange variations can sometimes make a difference. One of the assorted colors of the Wulff series can trigger feeding in trout. You don't need to go for subtle differences here, but there are times when color can be a key to feeding behavior.

An Old Reliable Box, containing the flies you use in 90 percent of mountain-water angling, is the fly box you reach for most often.

Size and color variations will help you in most sticky situations. If they fail, then change the general shape of the pattern you use. If the Humpy outline seems to be putting fish off, don't change to the similarly shaped Irresistible. Instead try a Brown Wulff or maybe a Parachute Adams. When all else fails, especially in the fall, try dark-colored flies.

The Old Reliable Fly Box

Before I got smart and stopped trying to match every hatch, I carried in my vest about 1,000 flies representing close to 200 patterns. There was a nymph box, a terrestrial box, a match-the-hatch box, and a wet-fly box. Because I was stubborn, it took a couple of years for me to realize that I was ignoring or not catching fish on 180 of those patterns and was relying on 20 patterns 90 percent of the time. When I figured out what was going on, I pulled the most useful patterns together in what I call my Old Reliable Box.

The Old Reliable Box is filled with patterns that share few characteristics with real insects. I don't choose them to please the fish, but patterns are placed in the box for what they do for me. They are proven flies that over time have instilled confidence. The Old Reliable Box is the easiest to get at because I use these flies about 80 percent of the time.

I spend winter evenings sitting in front of the fireplace refilling my depleted supply of Old Reliables. For mountain water, the basic list is the House and Lot, Parachute Adams, Parachute Brown Wulff, Ginger Dun Parachute, Royal Humpy, Renegade, Stimulator, Dry Muddler, Goddard Caddis, and Parachute Deer Hopper. Those ten flies are enough to see me through the majority of the action the following summer.

Patterns fall in and out of favor. Years ago, Elk Hair Caddis filled half of my Old Reliable Box, but then I switched to a Humpy in the same situations and swore it caught more fish. Humpys used to fill half the box, but the H and L has taken their place in most rough-water situations. Experience alters my favorites, and when I lose confidence in a pattern, I don't replace those flies when they wind up in the trees.

Every angler should develop a list of reliable patterns. Experiment to find what inspires your confidence in a fly pattern. Give unusual patterns a chance, as well as the ones everyone else seems to use. Make up your own Old Reliable Box, and put it in a handy vest pocket. Confidence in your choice of fly will lead to more fish on the end of your line.

One more thing about flies. Like most fly fishers, I prefer fishing with a dry fly. It's visual fishing, much like standing in a mountain stream is basically a visual experience. I'm also much better at fishing dries than nymphs. I've read time and again that trout take up to 90 percent of their food from the subsurface, and I don't doubt that's true. But opportunistic feeders are always on the watch for food and always seem willing to grab a floating fly. I can think of only a few instances in the summer when mountain trout took nymphs but not dry flies. Streams with thick populations of large stoneflies are an exception, so carrying stonefly nymph patterns is always a good idea. And it never hurts to throw in your pocket a few general attractor nymphs like Hare's Ear, Pheasant Tail, or Prince.

DESCARTES'S PARADOX AND MATCHING THE HATCH

Rene Descartes was a practical man. While the grand philosophers of his day were expressing universal doubt, Descartes was unflapped. *His* brain was working at full speed; thus, the simple basis of his philosophy—*Cogito, ergo sum.* To the rest of us, this became, "I think, therefore I am."

Descartes's pragmatism extended to his view of God and his fellow man. He couldn't understand those who doubted God's existence. In his mind, it was senseless to profess disbelief in the Creator.

"Why would anyone deny the existence of God?" Descartes wondered. If God existed and you were a believer, then you were covered. You got forgiveness and all that. But if there was a God and you didn't accept it, you were in trouble. So Descartes asked, "Why not hedge your bet?" Convince yourself to believe and you'll have nothing to lose.

Herein lies the paradox. If you were right in the first place and there was no God, it wouldn't matter, for there was no salvation anyway. If you were wrong, and there *was* a God, and if you said you believed, you'd be accepted by Him. So you can't lose if you say you believe in the Supreme Creator.

I was thinking about Descartes and his paradox last summer on the upper Rio Grande in the San Juan Mountains of Colorado. The summer thunderstorms had moved off for a couple of days and it was one of those rare, shining evenings when the tired sun casts nothing but orange light on the high divides. In a rare moment, trout were rising freely up and down the meadow stretch below camp, and all was right with the world.

Typically, I was throwing out a size 12 House and Lot to the trout that I saw. Nearly every cast brought a glint of trout from behind the stream-covered rocks, but only one in five brought a solid strike. Not the best of ratios, and tying on a size 14 of the same pattern didn't change a thing. I'm a pretty stubborn guy, and I refused to believe that it mattered to these trout—swimming in a river at 9,500 feet—what they were eating.

That's when Descartes came to mind. If I acted as if I believed that this was a case when matching the hatch was important, what difference would it make? If my original contention was correct, and the fish didn't pay all that much attention to what their potential food looked like, then fishing a hatch-matcher wouldn't matter. The fish would take it as readily as anything else. If I was wrong, and the fish were fussier than I'd like to admit, then I'd still be covered.

I scooped a couple of size 14, gray mayflies off the surface of a slow-moving pocket, then tied on a matching Adams. At first, the new fly didn't seem to make a difference, but gradually I had to admit that the fish were a bit bigger and were coming with a little more frequency. Maybe I was on to something?

Or maybe not. Who knows? When you are faced with one of the gray areas where the fish might be feeding selectively, don't hesitate to remember Descartes and the basic tenets of matching the hatch. It might not really matter, but what have you got to lose? Catch a few bugs, match them with a pattern, and see if you don't catch a few more trout.

Chapter Four

Freestone Streams: Mix and Match

Take a look at the gorgeous color photography in fly-fishing magazines, beer commercials, and travel guides to the western states. One subject dominates—clear water reflecting the deep blue sky and flowing swiftly around rocks. Study one of the shots. Gravel bars shove their way into the stream along one bank, pushing the stream hard up against the other. Off in the middle distance, the rollicking currents give way to a smooth surface where, as writers from the Greeks to modern times have observed, the water runs deep. In the foreground, no doubt, lies a big boulder sitting in the currents, forcing its will upon the waters. Like the sonata form applied by classical composers to support their music, the stream is a repeating sequence of similar structures—riffle, run, pool—with each reappearance offering a slight variation of the motif.

Most anglers would call such a place freestone water. I'm apt to get all dreamy-eyed and call it paradise. Freestone water defines a large proportion of mountain streams and makes up the most common type of rivers in the West.

Like a frugal woman's wardrobe, freestone streams are a mix-and-match collection of a few basic elements. The

READING A FREESTONE STREAM

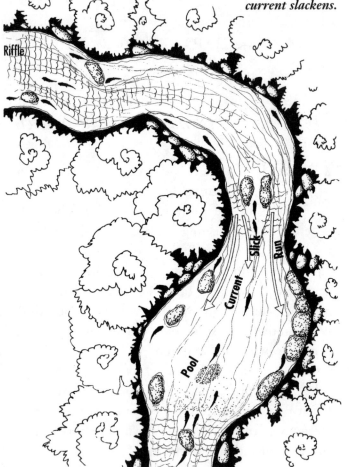

Riffles: Shallow water, plenty of insects. Fish may hold anywhere the current slackens.

Riffle

Slick

Current

Run

Pool

Pools: Deep, clear water. Fish sit deep or at head and tail of the pool. Don't forget the edges.

Runs and Slicks: Fish hold in slicks when the surface is smooth and the water is from 1–3 feet deep. Don't forget the current seams at the edges of slicks.

components of freestone streams are riffles, runs, pools, and slicks. Each ingredient is a different mix of water and rocks that results in variations in water depth and current speed. A gravel bottom is the underlying theme to the entire stream, and it is the rocks, both below the surface and poking through the film, that best characterize the water and give to it the endless variation of appearance, sound, and angling opportunity.

A freestone stream is a suite of water types linked by the melodies of the current. The stream gradient—determined by how steeply the water tumbles from the peaks—controls the relative amounts of riffle, run, and pool. Small creeks that drop straight down mountainsides are apt to be a series of cascades linked together like a string of white pearls. Lower-order streams, those that gather in the flow of the smallest tributaries, usually hold a greater percentage of riffles and runs. Of course, the underlying geology plays a role, too, and vanished glacial lakes may bring the flow to a screeching halt and create extensive meadows—essentially very long pools—smack dab in the middle of roaring canyons.

The overwhelming majority of mountain waters are classified as freestone streams. The basic trick to angling such water is to find the right water depth and speed that hold trout in each type of water. But first you need to readjust your thinking about how to cast your fly to the proper spot.

CASTING OFF OLD HABITS: FLIP AND RIVER CASTS

Casting videos are now as abundant as exercise tapes, suggesting ways to add inches to your fly line instead of taking them off your waistline. The films are almost universally excellent when it comes to instructing beginners on how to pump out line over smooth-flowing waters. If you want to learn how to throw a line as far as possible, go out and get one of these visual tools.

The problem is that no matter how graceful those long casts appear, they are absolutely unnecessary on mountain water. In fact, a long cast is a detriment on mountain streams because there are too many complications.

For the most part, casts *must* be short on mountain streams, small or large. If you have a lot of fly line on the water, the complex currents of mountain water—alternating slow and fast lanes—will quickly pull on the line and drag the fly across the surface. Short casts will keep your fly line off the water and prevent your fly from moving in an unnatural manner. Short casts will also help keep flies out of overhanging brush. Finally, short casts are required to properly manage the line as you must for successful fishing on fast-moving streams.

What the casting videos usually neglect are the alternate, simple casting techniques that are necessary on mountain waters. To be honest, the rod and line movements aren't pretty—they are sort of working-class variations of the theme of casting. Those picturesque closed loops, as well as false casting, are not required for mountain-water techniques like the flip and river casts.

The simplest yet most often used casting technique on mountain freestone streams is the flip cast. This cast, basically nothing more than a flick of the wrist, is the best method of making a short cast into mixed currents, or to work fly line in close quarters. It is ideal for working up the middle of small streams, covering brushy waters, or thoroughly fishing pocket water.

When the water is a mix of current seams, you want to target your fly within 10 or 12 feet of where you are standing. The flip cast is perfect for this. The goal of the flip cast is to hit a single, short current line or a pocket. To accomplish

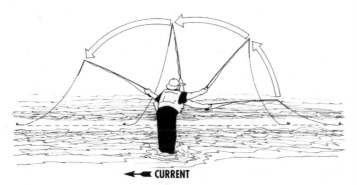

Drifting Dry Flies after a Flip Cast

← CURRENT

Very much like high-stick nymphing, the flip cast and drift will permit you to work a current lane without creating drag. Using only the leader and a short bit of fly line, flip the fly upstream and onto the current lane you want to explore. Once the fly is drifting on the water, keep the line tight, with only a tiny bit of slack, by raising the rod tip as the fly drifts downstream.

this, you want to fish with only the tippet, the leader, and 2 to 5 feet of fly line. The flip cast will direct your imitation to the target, allow you to control the float through the lie, and instantly set you up for the next cast.

Start by holding the rod at the 1 o'clock position. Have a short length of line extending from the rod tip—just enough to extend beyond the lie you want to cover. Let the fly drop to the water and allow the current to pull the line tight, loading the rod. Move the rod forward with a smooth motion, as if you were throwing a baseball. At the 11 o'clock position, add a sharp flick of the wrist and let the rod tip drop. The fly will head in a straight line to the target area—no muss, no fuss.

The second part of a flip cast is controlling the float of the fly. Once the fly is drifting on the water, keep the line tight, with only a tiny bit of slack, by using arm and rod movements.

The rod tip stays low at the beginning of the drift when the fly is farthest away. As the fly drifts toward you, lift your arm and rod to keep the line tight, then lower the rod again as the distance between you and the fly increases. You can also extend the drift a few feet by extending your arm out straight and leaning into the very end of the float. If this sounds a bit like the Leisenring Lift of nymph fishing, you're right.

When the line is pulled taut at the end of the drift, make another flip and repeat the process. On an average cast of 10 to 12 feet, the whole sequence takes less than ten seconds.

The simple beauty of the flip cast makes it ideal for beginning fly fishers. Because there is no slack line on the water, it's a one-handed technique that leaves the noncasting hand with nothing to do until a fish is on. With only one hand involved, the whole of angling becomes easier to manage.

When conditions require a bit more of a cast, say out to 15 or 20 feet, a flip of the wrist won't do. Then it's time for a variation of the flip cast that puts a bit more energy into the line and carries the fly farther. I watched New Mexico guide Barrie Bush teach this technique to novice fly fishers with great success, and he called it the river cast.

The river cast is an easy step up from the flip cast and, like that simple technique, eliminates the backcast, which is so often the trouble spot for those unfamiliar with confined casting quarters. Begin the same way as you do for the flip cast, but allow the fly to float downstream and tighten the line. You can adjust the length of the cast by changing the amount of line pulled out by the current. Then with a smooth motion and a broad sweep of your arm, pull the line off the water and send it upstream. Your motion should be a bit more vigorous than with the flip cast, and your arm should move quickly from the 2 o'clock to the 10 o'clock position.

Once the cast is made, you'll have to do a bit of line management. This is where your noncasting hand comes into play. The task of the free hand is to control slack and thus the tightness of the line. This is necessary, because it's difficult to set a hook with a limp line.

The easiest way to manage line is to drape it into your noncasting hand as soon as the cast is complete. Loosely grip the line between your thumb and the first couple of fingers. In most freestone stream situations, you want the line to stay tight so there is no slack line on the water. If you end up with slack line, pinch the line with your noncasting hand and hold constant the amount of line coming out of the rod. The line hand holds the fly line firmly, thus leaving the same length of line extending from the rod tip. As with the flip cast, you manage the line with arm and rod movements. Pinching the line in the fingers of your nonrod hand, start with a low rod, raise it as the fly floats by, and lower the rod as it passes.

More often than not, longer casts and stripping line mean you'll have to do a bit of mending of the line to keep the float going. Mending line requires more skill. You strip line more slowly from the water, then, with a rolling motion, you throw the slack line back upstream.

Once you make a cast in quick currents, you have a few seconds to use your rod to position the fly in the proper current lane. To move to a current line closer to you, just pull up on the rod tip. The fly will drag across the surface. In choppy water, however, this won't be noticeable to a fish 5 or 10 feet downstream.

GOING LONGER: STRAIGHT-LINE, REACH, AND S-CASTS

The attractive simplicity of the flip and river casts won't get you a trout in all situations. There are times when traditional casting is required—times when you need to go 20 or 30 feet or cross a series of complicated currents to get to the opposite bank. One situation where the quarter upstream cast is the perfect choice is on mid- to large-sized rivers with low gradients and no midstream boulders. Although they are not common in the mountains, such places do exist.

The straight-line cast is the standard of fly fishing. This is the cast to use when you need a long, drag-free float. A straight-line cast is ideal for working from within the stream and angling along the bank or along undercuts, or when you are working in pools. On freestone mountain water, it's the cast of choice when you are putting a fly on long runs and slicks. To get the best float, you usually want to aim the fly at the quarter upstream position; that is, a point halfway between directly upstream and directly across to the opposite bank. The mechanics of this cast have been thoroughly covered by other authors. On smooth, simple currents, this technique will yield a long drift through a single current lane.

Careful line management is often necessary when casts are more than 20 feet. Make a straight-line cast and drape the line into your free hand. Here you'll have to immediately begin stripping line with your nonrod hand. Pinch the line between your thumb and fingers and pull in a foot or so of line, just enough to keep only a little slack line on the water. Pull too much and the line goes taut and the fly drags; pull too little and you'll leave too much slack and probably miss the strike. Move the rod tip downstream, keeping it pointed roughly in the direction of the fly. At the same time, keep the line between your fingers and slide your hand up the line, back to a point near the rod, and be ready to give another strip. It's a fluid motion, sliding the hand up and down while slowly swinging the rod tip downstream. Once the line is downstream and pulling, you can make another cast, or you can allow line to slip back through your fingers to put more line on the water and lengthen the next cast.

More often than not in mountain water, the midstream rocks and the shape of the banks will interfere with the results of a straight-line cast. The line will cross current lanes that alternate fast and slow. In this situation, a straight fly line will quickly drag a fly out of the target lane and across the current. Not even mountain trout will be fooled by such an unnatural action on the part of a fly. A straight-line cast will not often work. Instead of a beeline between you and the fly, you need to introduce some slack into the line.

The easiest method of reducing drag on a long cast is to use a reach cast. Use the reach cast when a current lane of fast-moving water lies between you and the target lane where you expect to find trout. This situation is amazingly common on mountain streams and is most often the case when you are casting to the slow current lanes along the opposite bank. A straight-line cast in this setup will result in a fly line that drifts on the nearby, fast current, quickly pulling the fly from the target lane. You need to make a cast that places the bulk of the fly line on the water a few feet upstream of the fly. This will give the fly line a few seconds to catch up with and pass the fly, and those few seconds are all you need to permit the fly to float gently over your target. The reach cast does just that.

This simple variation of the straight-line cast adds only one step to the basic cast, making it easy to master. Set up as you would for a straight-line cast, targeting an area between a quarter upstream and directly opposite your location. Have 2 or 3 feet of additional line out than you would need for a straight-line cast to the target. Begin a standard cast, sending the fly on a straight line to your target. As the line straightens out, but before it drops to the water, take your arm and swing it 2 feet in the upstream direction. Reach with your arm across your body. Don't raise the rod tip, and at the end of the reach, lower your arm and allow the line to settle on the water. If all goes well, the leader, the tippet, and the fly will continue on a straight course and hit the target, while most of the line will float several feet upstream. Depending

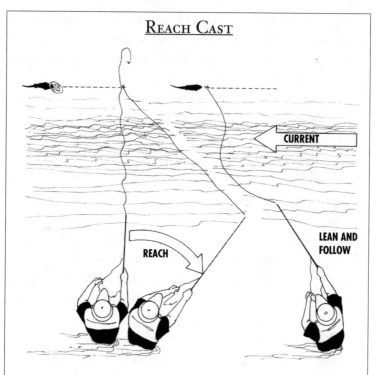

REACH CAST

CURRENT

LEAN AND FOLLOW

REACH

Use the reach cast when a current lane of fast-moving water lies between you and the target lane where you expect to find trout. 1) Make a straight-line cast directly opposite of your location, but with a bit of extra line in the cast. 2) As the line straightens out, but before it drops to the water, take your arm and swing it upstream. Lower your arm and allow the line to settle on the water. 3) Follow the line with the rod when the line straightens out as it reaches your target.

on the speed of the intervening current, you will have 2 to 10 seconds of drag-free float before the line overtakes the fly and begins to pull the pattern from the target current lane.

When there is only one change in current between you and your target, the reach cast is all you need. However, you will frequently find yourself in streams where there are multiple current lanes between you and that desired feeding lane against the bank or around a rock. A reach cast will help, but the numerous speed changes on the line between you and the fly will pull the pattern away from any hungry trout. More slack is necessary.

It's time for the most complex mountain-water cast, the S-cast. The S-cast will serve you well when you are making long casts across turbulent, complex flow. Maybe you can guess the reason from the name—the goal of the cast is to have the fly line lying on the water in a series of Ss. And it's not as difficult as it might seem.

The S-cast adds two steps to the basic straight cast. Stand as you would for a straight-line cast, in the standard quarter upstream position. Target your fly a couple feet upstream from the suspected lie. Strip off 2 or 3 more feet of fly line than it takes to reach the target. Begin the cast as you normally would, continuing up to the point where you've begun the forward cast and the fly is heading toward the target. Hesitate a half-second, then check the forward motion of your arm, stopping short of the usual 10 o'clock position. As the line heads toward the water to settle on the surface, give the rod tip a couple of horizontal shakes. The motion will take the line and drop it on the water in a series of curves. The different currents will take up the curves and leave the fly sliding along its merry way, if only for a few critical seconds, in the proper feeding lane.

THE PANTRY: RIFFLES

If you can execute the proper mountain-water techniques required by the tricky currents of rocky, tumbling streams, all you have to do is find the fish and you're in business.

Given the opportunity to spread out over a wide area, a stream will thin to form shallows where the water trips over thousands of rocks to form riffles. Water depths range from 6 inches to as much as 3 feet, but most riffles stay in the area

A regular rhythm of broken water makes up a riffle, where insect life is abundant.

of 12 inches. The current runs fast, barely impeded as it pushes over the small- to medium-sized rocks. Because the water doesn't have much depth, you can see the shape of the bottom by looking at the surface, like a child unsuccessfully trying to hide under a blanket.

Riffles can be a good place to cast your flies because they offer trout two of their three basic requirements. The well-oxygenated, shallow water allows plenty of light to penetrate, and algae grows in profusion on the subsurface rocks. The algae serves as a food base for large populations of aquatic insects—particularly nymphs that cling to the surface of rocks—which, in turn, are fed on by trout. Fulfilling another need, the rock fields create hundreds of small areas of slack water that offer trout a break from the full force of the current. Put these factors together and you'll find large numbers of trout.

Riffles aren't perfect, however. Most pockets of slack water are small and, as a whole, riffles are too shallow to offer trout good protection from predators. So while there are plenty of them, most trout feeding in riffles are small—less than 12 inches. That's not to say you should treat riffles lightly. It's not uncommon to find a truly large fish getting a suntan on his back while feeding on the rich insect life in a riffle. Because of the numbers of trout, riffles are an ideal spot for beginners to fish. Even old hands can have a blast fishing there.

It is considered proper to fish a riffle with discipline and hard work—a task that requires, if not the patience of Job, at least that of his son. Start at the tail of the riffle and use a flip, river, or straight line cast to reach the currents fairly close to where you are standing. If nothing happens, cast out a couple feet farther. Remember that in choppy water, trout can't really see very far. Make your next cast a few feet beyond the last one until you cover the width of the stream. Then move a couple of steps upstream and repeat the process. You're sure to find some fish with this methodical approach.

I'm usually not so patient. I prefer to dissect the riffle. I look for the best water and am stingy with my casts like a miser with his pennies. It's the cast-benefit ratio—an economy of casts, directed toward where I suspect I might find a better fish. Holding lies along the bank or instream logs are prime candidates to receive a cast. Big midstream rocks that push up a large cushion of slack water get a lot of my attention. I also watch for subtle signs of slightly deeper water— a bluish tint to the water or a patch of smooth surface. I direct most of my attention to such spots, and often that's where I find a nice trout. Most of the time I use a flip cast to reach the target, but a reach cast is useful for hitting pockets upstream from rocks and when fishing behind nearby rocks.

In their moments of respite, the streams deepen and calm, forming picturesque pools and creating perhaps the most inviting spots on a river. If you weren't a fisherman you'd call them swimming holes—the only places where the depth is over your head. In clear mountain water, you can often pick out individual rocks on the bottom of a pool through 8 feet of water. Because pools are worthy destinations simply because of their beauty, it's okay to forget about trout for awhile.

Pools are great spots for angling in mountain water. Not only are they inviting to look at, but usually a couple of big trout are lurking around the bottom of pools, while a host of smaller groupies are hanging around the edges. At the head of a pool is a spot where food drops in, riding on the currents from above. Trout frequently hang out there. On the opposite end, at the tail of the pool, the channel constricts and funnels food through the narrowing flow. Trout often work the tail of the pool.

The trick of angling in a pool is getting to the fish. The surface of a pool is an exposed place for trout. Because the glassy water offers no protection, the trout try to hide near the bottom or along the edges of the pool. The clarity of the water and the depth of the pool conspire to make angling a difficult prospect. The trout have all the advantages here.

You can make angling a pool as easy or as complex as you wish. For the small pools of mountain water, I recommend starting at the tail, fishing the depths, then hitting the far bank, and finally casting to the head of the pool.

The deep water and glassy surface of the tail of a pool require that you approach with some caution or the fish will scatter. You need to keep your silhouette and your fly rod back from the pool, requiring you to cast over the faster currents of whatever water lies directly below the pool. On small streams, it's best to use a flip cast from directly below the pool

Quiet-flowing pools often shelter the biggest trout in a stream.

and keep your rod tip high enough so that the fly line remains off the water. You can usually do this by casting and then holding the butt of your rod in front of you, over your head. This gives you a few seconds of float through the critical area. In larger pools, it's easier to approach the tail of the pool from the side, along the bank. Keep a low profile, use as few rod movements as possible, and make a reach cast or an S-cast out to the tail of the pool.

The largest trout in a pool are probably hanging out near the bottom, picking nymphs from the rocks under the cover of the depths. To challenge the big ones, you need to scrape your flies along the bottom or close to it. The fish can use the protection of the rocks down there, so they may be found anywhere in the pool. You must drop nymph patterns quickly through deep water—not an easy proposition. It takes a good bit of weight on the leader about a foot up from the fly. The best type of weight is the nonlead, doughball type that you can mold to any size and shape and squeeze onto your leader.

Stand as far from the head of the pool as possible and use a straight-line cast to toss the weighted fly and leader near the head of the pool. Reach with your arm to keep the fly line off to the same side from which you are casting. It takes patience to find the amount of weight necessary to get the fly to the bottom. Drift the fly through the entire pool, then make a slow retrieve to the bank. The fly has a lot of sinking to do to get to the bottom, and many pools just aren't long enough to allow the fly to sink. In this case, go with wet flies fished as deep as you can comfortably get them.

Once you've exhausted the possibilities in the center of the pool, make some casts to the opposite side, drifting flies along the rocks as you would in any other stream situation. You may have to use a reach cast or S-cast to deal with the various currents of the pool.

The point where fast water eases to a near standstill is the head of the pool. You'll find a few fish there, especially in the morning and evening when there are plenty of bugs on the water. It's straightforward angling, using flip casts and drifting dry flies over the first few feet of the slow water. Keep the line off the water as much as possible, or cast so that the line stays along the bank on the same side from which you cast. If there's a low waterfall at the head of the pool, keep your fly out of the foaming water. Use a high rod to place your fly on the lines of smooth current between the foam.

OFF AND RUNNING: RUNS AND SLICKS

In between the character of riffle and the pool are spots called runs. These are places where streams ease down a drop in elevation, not with a tumble, but with a quick-moving, bobbing surface. The flow is rarely broken into foam, but the current is not still. Runs are kind of like fast-moving pools.

A run squeezed against a rock offers deeper water and often harbors decent trout.

When they are long and broad, these stretches are called flats, but the mountain-water angler will find few of these on smaller streams.

The secret of a run lies in its depth, near the bottom. With water moving swiftly through the run, friction along the bottom creates a balloon of slower water just above the gravel. Trout can hold near the bottom, get a break from the currents, and watch above for food floating on the currents.

Runs show up where the current is forced up against rocky banks, along grassy shores, and in stretches where rocks are scattered. Basic runs can range from 12 inches to many feet in depth. In the shallower sections, trout lack protection, and you won't find many hanging around. What you are looking for are channels within the run where the water is 18 inches or more deep. In runs, the guiding principle is "everything in moderation." Look for places with moderate current speeds

A slick is a quiet flow sandwiched between two faster current lanes.

and water depths. Use flip casts and S-casts to get your fly floating along the channels.

Related to the run is the one type of mountain water for which fly fishers should always be on the watch—slicks. Slicks are spots where fairly deep water glides along with a smooth surface, often forming a repeating pattern of small waves. Slicks are almost a combination of a riffle and a run. To form a slick, the flow of the stream is usually constricted between two features like rocks, a bank, logs, or two very different types of current. Any of these features will give the speed of the current a little boost, channeling food items through the constriction. Thus, slicks are often chutes that lie between unimportant currents.

Because the water is deeper in a slick, the surface isn't broken as it is in a riffle. The stream bottom is a jumble of rocks, both large and small. Underwater cobbles are small or too far from the surface to create a break in the surface flow. But the subsurface rocks can create swells and troughs on the surface above. You have to pay some attention to the currents to pick out the slicks. Look for bubbles that are gliding down a tongue of current faster than those on either side. Usually, larger forces—gravel bars, two-ton rocks, or deeply grooved bottom channels—squeeze together the lines of current, making the water slide downstream a little faster and deepening the flow, but not too much.

The slicks often hold the stream's best fish. They offer trout protection from predators and fast currents, as well as a constant supply of food. This is most true in water that is 12 to 18 inches deep, and if you find such a slick, you're in for some great angling.

WORKING THE WATER (SOMEBODY'S GOT TO DO IT)

I'm not the first to observe that fly fishing has much in common with sex—anticipation is half the fun.

Stepping off the bank and into the swirling waters of the Rio Guadalupe, my skin tingled from the top of my head to my toes. The narrow river was classic freestone water— boulders plopped midstream, breaking the flow into tongues of current moving in all directions, a patchwork of riffles fading into pools, rolling runs, and a backdrop of sheer canyon walls dotted with pines clinging to the cracks. A quick scan of the scene told me that from each casting location in the river, I could drop a fly to a dozen spots that would likely hold a trout. It was a fishy river, and I would be happy to spend the morning there anticipating a trout in each of the hundreds of lies in a quarter-mile stretch. Even if I didn't land a single fish, the variety and sheer number of places to cast would keep me interested. I couldn't ask for anything more.

An angler properly working a stretch of freestone water is always on the move and constantly casting. This doesn't

Choppy water permits you to get in close to your target and use easy-to-execute flip casts.

mean you have to cover a lot of water, but a lot of lies. With a dazzling array of potential trout lies in which typically only 25 percent hold fish, you need to try hundreds of lies in the course of the day.

The action—although not necessarily the trout action—is fast on freestone water. You are constantly casting to likely spots, and the water hustles the fly right back to you. In many situations, a cast is followed by five seconds of drift. Then it's time to retrieve your fly and cast again. The whole cycle may take no more than eight seconds.

In such a situation, step into the water and get prepared for comfortable casting. If you are right-handed, position yourself a few steps in from the left bank as you are facing upstream. This will keep your rod over the water and decrease your chance of an uncalled-for encounter with the willows and alders. Find a spot on the stream bottom where your footing is stable and the currents aren't tugging at your calves, trying to force you a few steps closer to salt water.

Cast to the nearest spot most likely to harbor trout. If necessary, adjust your cast with a few arm movements to put the fly on the proper current. Drift your fly over the likely lie and any others that hang on the same current, then retrieve the pattern and immediately cast again to the same spot. Repeat the sequence once or twice, but don't put in a lot of time on the same lie. The most common mistake made by beginners on mountain water is making too many casts to the same spot. If nothing happens—a flash, a hit, or a take—on the first two drifts, nobody's home, or any trout in the hole isn't interested in your offering. It's time to move on. When a lie comes up empty, look for the next one—perhaps a rock a bit farther out or a run a few feet upstream.

From any given casting location, hit the spots progressively farther out to avoid disturbing any lies with the line before they are tested. Extend your casting out as far as you can without disrupting the float. On a good freestone stream, you can hit a half-dozen lies from a single casting spot.

Once you've played out the lies from one casting spot, move upstream about 10 feet and find another stable casting platform. As you move upstream, you can either stay to the left or right bank, or, if the stream is wide and shallow, head up the middle of the flow. From the middle, you can keep your casts short, hit your targets more accurately, and access the prime lies that sit along both banks. Casting from the center of the stream will also help keep your flies out of the trees.

You may have to do a bit of backhand casting to cover the water effectively. Backhand flip casts will permit you to work both banks of a stream and in other situations will help keep your flies out of the trees. The casting stroke is a lot like a tennis player's backhand. Move your rod arm across your body, allow the line to drift behind you, then swing your

The deep water against the rock creates a run, where you'll often find good trout.

forearm forward and give your wrist a snap. The cast plays out like a flip cast. Use the backhand cast when there is thick brush close behind you.

Pick and choose your spots, ignoring water that seems unlikely to hold a trout. This means that you might walk upstream 20 yards before making the next series of casts. If you are making just a few steps of advance, you can false cast on the way. If you must walk farther, pull in the fly, hold it in your nonrod hand, and head upstream.

Keep your casts short so that you never have a lot of line on the water. Because freestone water fly fishing means hitting as many lies as you can, you need to be on the move constantly. You should be able to move upstream without reeling in a lot of line. Manage your line with your hands.

Preparation of the dry fly can also affect the float. Give the pattern a healthy dose of fly floatant—the size of a big teardrop—that will cover the hackle, the body, the tail, and even the wings of the fly. The wings will get soaked, and you want to be able to bring the fly back to the surface on the next cast. When a fly gets tired, dry it off on your shirttail or other cloth and send it on its way again. Re-coat it with floatant as needed. You should, however, be able to use a bushy fly for half an hour without stopping to treat it.

It's not easy to put into words how to work a nice drift in complex currents. After awhile, instincts take over and you are unaware of just what it is you do to stretch out a float.

While teaching a class of beginners the basics of finding fish in rolling currents, I did a little demonstration. I cast a Humpy to a small current seam lying against the far bank of the Pecos River. I figured that one of the long pieces of limestone near the shore would hide a fish. I did the standard reach cast, drifting the fly in a nice line past the first rock. It was such a nice float, I decided to let the fly swing by the next rock farther downstream. As the Humpy got close, I was running out of slack, so to extend the float, I stretched my arm as far toward the other bank as it would go. Even with that, I needed another foot to reach the prime lie in front of the rock. I bent at the waist, leaning far over the river. It was an awkward position, with my butt sticking out, my torso twisted, and my arm fully extended. It gave me just enough additional float and the fly disappeared in a swirl. One of the students yelled, "You never mentioned anything about contortion."

Use your arm and its extension—your fly rod—to make minor adjustments to the drift that will put the fly where you want it. This technique can be used to place a fly on a current tongue, into a pocket, to extend a drift a few inches into the perfect spot, or to avoid a current that would take the fly from its intended drift.

As your fly drifts on the water, you'll have to keep a close watch to follow its path. It helps to have a sense of just where

By holding your rod up high, you can keep all the fly line off the water, allowing the leader to drift along a single current lane.

the fly is going in the first place—a skill that can only be developed with practice. It's inevitable that occasionally, or even often, the fly will get lost amid the rocks, foam, bubbles, and currents. That doesn't mean you'll lose a fish, however, if you bring all your senses into the game. Pay close attention to the feel of your line. Like nymphing, any tug or sudden motion of your line or leader could mean a hit. Don't hesitate to strike. Listen for a splashy rise, and strike if you hear one. Perhaps the best indicator of a hit in a hidden fly is the flash of a fish—a darting silver reflection often means a hit. When your fly should be moving through a prime location and you don't want to waste a drift through it due to a lost fly, tighten up a bit on the line. The motion of the fly will often induce a strike from a trout, and the tight line will more likely lead to a hook-up.

Mountain Rhythms

Amid the swirling passage of my days and the uncertainty of the future of our species, I turn to the mountains to restore my sense of balance between what is important and what is drivel. I gain reassurance in the repeating cycles of nature, especially ones that extend beyond the rising and setting of the sun and the slide from warm days to cold ones—the cycles that I can't experience from my personal retreat among the lawn and flowerbeds of my yard. I need to know that no matter what happens in my day-to-day world, I'll find calypso orchids beneath the Douglas firs in June and a yellow bathtub-ring of pine pollen on the lakes in July, that thunder will echo from the peaks in August, and that frost will cover the coffeepot in mid-September. There is much comfort, too, in finding Green Drakes on the Rio Grande in late June or thumb-sized grasshoppers on the Piedra River around my birthday in late August.

To the angler, the general mountain rhythms are predictable like the quiet beat of a soothing song. You can count on summer thunderstorms bringing a welcome cloud cover that will encourage mayfly hatches and improve the catch. Golden stoneflies will stimulate trout feeding after runoff on many streams. Caddis flies will be productive in the evening. But beyond knowing what will happen within broad ranges of time, trying to pinpoint when events will occur is as shaky as walking on the ground surrounding an old beaver pond.

The variability of seasonal and daily weather patterns at high elevations can play havoc with nature's schedule. There are no well-established patterns that don't have frequent exceptions. Angling mountain water always means exploring, probing, and investigating the environment. It's a constant learning process in which every cast explores new territory. You have to approach such water with an open mind and with no preconceptions as to what will happen there. For many reasons, each mountain-water trip is an adventure into the unknown.

One mountain rhythm that is worth careful observation is the timing of runoff. If you can predict when runoff will begin and end, you can let yourself in for some fantastic pre-runoff angling and prevent a wasted trip to a muddy torrent that in a couple weeks would be a decent trout stream.

Three major factors determine when and how much a stream will run off each spring—depth of snowpack, spring temperatures, and the characteristics of the watershed. Because these factors vary from watershed to watershed, runoff in each is unique. The interplay of factors means that nearby streams within the same mountain range can exhibit radically different patterns of runoff.

The depth of winter snowpack in the mountains drained by a stream determines how much water will be channeled through the riverbed when the thaw begins. There's no doubt that winter snowfall in the Rockies is highly variable and can range from not much more than a dusting to seasons with monumental snow depths. Keeping an eye on the ski reports will give you some idea of how much snow is in the mountains. The amount of snow will tell you how high the rivers will run.

The timing of runoff is largely determined by spring temperatures. Cool springs help keep the snow in the mountains longer, delaying the start of runoff. The slow melt will prolong high-water conditions. Not only will the start of runoff be delayed, but runoff will end later.

The opposite condition, a warm spring, brings rapid melting. The large volume of water has little time to soak into the ground, causing a high percentage to wash down the slopes directly into streams. This fast-moving water picks up plenty of soil and rock, creating muddy stream conditions. Thus, warm spring temperatures create high, turbid runoffs that begin and end quickly.

The characteristics of the watershed drained by the stream also affect the timing of the runoff. The size of the watershed determines how much snow can accumulate in the winter and thus the volume of water that must leave in the spring. Small watersheds run off quickly and are likely to bring the first good angling of the year—as early as late May. Larger watersheds have a more prolonged runoff and won't be fishable until mid-July. The type of vegetative cover in the watershed is also important. Streams that flow through large meadows tend to run off fast and muddy. Watersheds draining forested slopes tend to run off late, but they remain clear.

The elevation and orientation of the watershed also influence the timing of runoff. Snow melts slowly at higher elevations, and the effect is prolonged if the watershed has predominantly north-facing slopes. Here in New Mexico, the Rio Santa Barbara is a classic example. The river runs a straight course from south to north and runoff often lingers to mid-July. But the water runs clear.

Of course, these factors don't exist in isolation. A warm spring with low snow is different that a warm spring with lots of snow. The interplay of the various factors makes predicting runoff challenging and fun.

Daily rhythms are a bit more dependable. Mayfly hatches occur at their prescribed hour, especially if there's a cloud cover. Caddis flies swarm in the afternoon, and trout never eat hoppers for breakfast. Lakes fish best in the morning and evening, but stream trout will feed throughout the day. In the summer, thunderstorms, or at least puffy clouds, will hide the sun for part of the afternoon.

One daily variation that is often overlooked is water temperature, particularly on high streams. One July weekend, I was taking a look at Brewster Park, a long meadow only a dozen miles from the source of the Rio Grande in the San Juan Mountains of Colorado. It's always difficult to contain my enthusiasm when exploring a new location, so I was on the water by 9 A.M. The freestone water was filled with likely trout spots, and a thin hatch of mayflies bobbed over the river. I made a hundred casts in the next two hours without so much as a look from the trout, if there were any, that lived there. Rather disappointed, by 11 A.M. I was ready to pack up and head downstream when I got my first hit on a Parachute Red Quill.

"Maybe these are fussier trout than I thought," I said to myself. I searched the willows and the air for anything that looked like a red quill natural, but all I saw were yellow sallies. Suddenly, fish were rising all around me. The Red Quill brought a few more fish, as did a smaller Yellow Stonefly dry, and then a Humpy, a House and Lot, and the usual mountain-water flies.

It was as if someone had turned on the feeding switch. The river went from dead to fantastic in the space of ten minutes. Over lunch, I searched my knowledge of trout streams for a factor that could bring about such a sudden, radical change. It had to be temperature. I checked the current status with my pocket thermometer—52 degrees. Before I left the park early the next morning, I poked my thermometer in again—45 degrees at 7:30 A.M.

You don't have to get up at the crack of dawn to catch fish on mountain water. You can be a lazy fly fisher, sleep late, linger over a second cup of coffee, and hit the water by 10:30 A.M. and not miss much action. Spend that extra time around camp enjoying the mountain rhythms as they unfold around you.

Chapter Five

Picking Pockets

W hen the steep trail finally crests the last hill of the canyon, the view of First Meadows of Elk Creek in southern Colorado is like a cooling shower washing away all your worries. A waterfall threads through the trees on the opposite canyon wall. Between ridges decked out in aspen and fir is a flat-bottomed valley filled with vibrant green grasses. Elk Creek makes slow, lazy turns across the meadow, its surface as smooth as polished ice. Most tantalizing are the tree-ring circles rippling across the surface, left by rising trout.

It's an idyllic scene—except for the dozen anglers who usually thrash at the half-mile stretch of sluggish water. Like most anglers, they are pulled by the magic of the meadow, fooled by the aching beauty of the flats into thinking they will catch lots of huge fish.

As I dropped into the meadow for an overnighter, I met a couple of anglers on their way out. They were glum and complained that they had fished all afternoon and hadn't hooked a trout. I expressed my sympathy, but I was not surprised or discouraged. I had another destination in mind.

I pitched my tent in a thin stand of Douglas fir near the upper end of the meadow. A couple hundred feet above, Elk Creek exits a three-mile stretch of tumbling cascades in a canyon—the antithesis of the meadow water below. Despite the throng downstream, I knew I'd have the canyon to myself. Camp chores completed, I cast a meaty Parachute Brown Wulff into the first deep run I came across, and it was promptly slammed by a feisty 12-inch wild brown. He was the first of more than thirty fish that came to my flies in the next two hours, including a fine 15-inch rainbow sipping mayflies in the shade of an overhanging spruce.

Given a choice between quiet meadow water and a high-gradient cascade, most anglers opt for the calmer water. They don't know what they're missing. Rock-choked, waterfall-laden, over-the-boulder streams broken by pillows of slack—pocket water—are some of the most overlooked and productive water on any stream. Yet, the careful study of pocket water is a neglected art.

Classic pocket water is characterized by submerged and above-the-surface rocks that disrupt a stream's flow almost everywhere. The result is a patchwork of stone, foam, and merging currents, along with pillows of slack. The same effect is produced on smaller mountain streams that jump from rock to rock over low waterfalls into plunge pools and that are squeezed between boulders. In both cases, the potholed streambed creates an abundance of sheltering lies for fish.

For most fly fishers, the churning surface is bewildering—a helter-skelter collection of moving water. But fishing pockets is the most straightforward of all types of fly fishing and surprisingly requires only basic skills. Casts and drifts can be ridiculously short, so there's no need to be an expert caster. Fly selection is always unimportant. Armed with a little knowledge of how to read the complex currents and find out where trout might be hiding, beginners can experience immediate success.

Huge boulders, swirling currents, and foaming water characterize pocket water.

The mountains are full of such water. Most small head-water streams hold stretches of pocket water as they tumble from snow-covered peaks with high stream gradients as much as 200 feet per mile. We're talking rugged canyons sliced into the peaks. On large rivers, pockets can be 10 feet deep, and the in-stream rocks can be the size of a pickup truck. You'll find water like this on long stretches of the Rio Grande in Colorado and New Mexico, on the Roaring Fork, and on the Gunnison River. Big pocket water is found on the rivers of Yellowstone country, such as the Gallatin and the Madison. In the Northwest, the Deschutes, the Umpqua, and the Salmon rivers offer anglers pocket after pocket. A common feature of these fisheries is that they are tumultuous, rugged streams holding wild trout.

When you first look at a piece of pocket water, it strikes you as being as frothy as the head on a well-crafted pale ale. Tumbling and swirling water cascades over rocks and around boulders that have fallen from slopes or from cliffs above. The flow is forced to slide through narrow gaps, where it picks up speed. Currents merge as often as freeways in Los Angeles. Your initial impression is that the conditions are too extreme for trout.

Take a closer look at a single flow line. The current goes from fast to slow in a short horizontal distance, its momentum broken by a rock. When its speed drops suddenly, the stream deepens, and—here is the key part—a small pillow of slack water forms. But it's not just one pillow—another small cushion develops on the downstream side of the rock. Even better, submerged rocks do the same thing in a more subtle manner.

In the turbulent water of small mountain streams, cascades are strung together like a bunch of pearls. Low waterfalls form where the main flow dives over barriers of stone. At the foot of the falls, the current backs up in a plunge pool—really just a big pocket of slack.

The paradox of pocket water is that amid all the dominant foam, the pockets of slack water are what hold the trout. Cushions of slack water surrounded by quick currents offer trout all they need. Falling water constantly mixes with the air and therefore is well oxygenated. The mixing currents are a conveyor belt carrying food, and the slack-water pockets provide protected lies. A trout can sit in quiet water and make quick forays into the currents to grab something to eat.

Pocket water provides fly fishers with several important advantages that make fishing there relatively easy, even for beginners. Trout in pocket water are likely to be insect feeders

To find the fish in pocket water, you must find the quiet pillows of slack backed up behind and in front of rocks.

and will readily take dry flies. Better still, the trout must make quick decisions about anything floating by that resembles food, and they are never selective feeders. From a pocket, a strike from a trout is fast and hard.

Rocks and the broken, choppy surface reduce the fish's field of vision, allowing anglers to get in close to the fish. You can pluck memorable trout from a pocket only a few feet away.

Life isn't perfect, and pocket water has one disadvantage. If you are looking for a trophy trout, you would do better to cast elsewhere. In creeks and small rivers, pocket fish range between 8 and 12 inches, and in large rivers they are usually less than 14 inches. Of course, there are exceptions to this rule. Deep pockets in the Rio Grande or the Madison may hide fat trout up to 22 inches.

In pocket water you can often catch a memorable trout that sits only a few feet away.

Long Rods and Stout Leaders

The complexity of currents in a stretch of pocket water means that a fly will be jostled around like a Cessna in a thunderstorm. The challenge is to get your fly to follow a natural drift through the myriad of swirls. It won't take years of experience to figure out that a long length of fly line on the water will make a drag-free drift impossible. Why? Because you want to put your fly where the fish are—in the slow-moving slack—and chances are, two or three faster currents will sit between you and your target pocket. If your fly line crosses these currents, your fly will drag as quickly as a grasshopper jumps.

The problem is easily solved by manipulating your fly line with your rod. A successful float through a pocket can be accomplished by using the fly rod to lift much or all of the fly line from the surface. When only the leader and tippet are on the water, the fly will float in a natural manner.

In pocket water, a rod is not used to make long casts. It is an extension of your arm that allows you to reach across currents and place a fly in a specific pocket or current line. A flip, a whip, or a short roll cast is all you need. The basic mountain-stream setup is ideal for most pocket water. A 5-weight line is well suited to flip casting, allowing you to power the line with a simple twist of the wrist.

Pocket-water trout are not tippet shy. You can work with a short leader from 6 to 8 feet long, depending on the width of the stream and the tightness of the streamside vegetation. If you use tippet lighter than 5X, be prepared to lose a few fish that will easily snap it against rocks. Don't worry—the choppy surface permits you to use tippet two sizes larger than you might normally feel appropriate, and 3X to 4X tippet is a good weight with which to start.

Trout that sit in pockets do not often feed selectively, so matching naturals is unimportant. You'll find a variety of fast-water, clinger mayflies and lots of stoneflies from big Salmon Flies to size 16 Little Green Stones. Dry flies should be large, high floaters, such as heavy-hackled or hair-bodied flies. Wulffs, Humpys, and Stimulators are pocket-water flies.

Nymphs are also effective in pockets. Patterns must be weighted to sink quickly in the swift currents, or you can add some weight to the leader 6 to 12 inches above the fly. Because the trout are not selective, attractor nymphs are well suited to pocket water. Standard patterns such as the Gold-Ribbed Hare's Ear, the All Purpose, or the Pheasant Tail are fine choices. Simple peacock-bodied flies, such as the Brown-Hackle Peacock and Zug Bug, are also effective. Patterns made with flashy synthetic materials are a good choice when the water is murky or the weather is hot.

Trout will often hit a fast-moving nymph hard, so it is

possible to be successful just drifting subsurface patterns through pockets. To see more subtle takes, use a strike indicator. Depending on the depth of the pocket, place the indicator on the tippet from 9 to 18 inches above the fly, increasing the distance in large rivers where pockets are deep. Another method is to use a dropper rig in pockets. Tie on a high-floating dry fly like a Humpy or an Irresistible. Add a 12- to 18-inch dropper of stout tippet tied to the bend of the hook. For the trailing fly, use a weighted size 16 to 18 attractor nymph—a Gold-Ribbed Hare's Ear or a Pheasant Tail will do. With this system, you double your chance of success on each cast.

Using the Long Arm

In pocket water, you almost always have to search for hidden trout. Rise forms disperse quickly in the fast currents. You may, however, catch the flash of a trout's flanks as it darts quickly to the surface for an insect and then dives again to his protected location.

The careful study of a single pocket will tell you how to approach fishing every pocket you find. Put a boulder about 3 feet in diameter in the middle of a stream flowing about 18 inches deep. At least a foot of stone juts above the surface of the water. As the current flows toward the rock, the obstruction divides the flow so that two current lanes develop, one on either side of the rock. Immediately in front of the rock, the water hits the solid object and gently falls back on itself. This creates a nice pocket of calm water a couple of feet wide. You'll often find a nice trout lying there, taking advantage of the slow current and feeding on the insects that drift by on the faster currents to each side.

As the current lanes on either side of the rock flow by it, they converge several feet downstream. Just how far downstream they join depends on the size of the boulder. Between

POCKET-WATER ROCK

Each of the hundreds of midstream rocks in pocket water creates several pillows of slack water where trout are likely to sit, waiting for food to float by. Fish will lie in the cushion of slack pushed up in front of the rock, in the calm pocket behind the rock, and in any slicks formed as the current slides beyond the rock.

the rough triangle created by the merging currents and the rock itself lies a large pocket of slack water. Trout take up feeding stations within the slack water, watching the currents and whatever food they carry slide by on either side. There is often

Behind a rock the current is slow, but along the sides are lines of faster water; hold the rod high to keep the line out of the faster water.

more than one trout in such a pocket, but the trout are usually smaller than the trout lying in front of the same boulder.

For every boulder, you have two places to place a fly—in the pocket in front, and in the pocket behind. A straight-line cast won't often produce results, however. Between you and every pocket lie those faster currents sliding around the sides of the boulder. You need to cast your fly into the slack water, then keep it there for a couple of seconds. A reach cast can do this for you. Aim the fly to hit the pocket, then before the line hits the water, reach upstream with your arm and let the line fall there. This will give you the necessary time for an effective float in the calm water of the pocket. This technique works very well for the pocket in front of a boulder.

The slack water behind a boulder is often 15 or 20 feet in length, which means that you need a longer float to effectively cover the prime water. It is necessary to hold the rod high to avoid dragging the fly with line that rides on the intervening faster current. In this case, it is best to work your way within 8 or 10 feet of the pocket. Make a flip cast to the slack water in the center of the pocket. Immediately hold your rod up over your head, pointing in front of you toward the fly. Keep the fly line off the water, holding only the fly and a bit of leader on the surface. Follow the drift downstream with your rod, watching carefully for the strike. Drift the fly for as long as you can before retrieving it and casting again, and vary the location of the drift within the pocket. Remember to float your fly along the current seams between the fast and slow water.

Pockets don't usually come singly, but in swarms. Before you make your first cast, study the surface of the stream and locate likely lies. Trout won't usually sit in mixing currents, so you can ignore areas of foam. Search for slower and deeper water—the pockets of slack water pushed up in front of rocks, smooth-surfaced miniruns or slicks between rocks, deep plunge pools, and spots where a hidden bowl on the bottom might protect a trout.

Don't be satisfied with just any lie. Search for prime locations where slow currents are adjacent to food lines. One such spot is between two surface-breaking rocks that sit parallel to the current. If the downstream boulder lies near the place where the two current lines from the upstream rock converge, there's almost always a nice trout lying in the pillow of water pushed up by the downstream rock. Another trout is often found in the head of the same pocket just below the upper rock.

When you have selected the most promising lie, step up to the stream and prepare to cast. Take advantage of the broken and choppy surface and get up close to the target. You can easily get as close as a rod's length away. Use rocks, submerged logs, and foam to screen yourself from the trout.

PLUNGE-POOL POCKET

The deepened flow created at the foot of a small plunge pool creates protection for trout, and fish will often hold there, especially if there are downstream rocks pushing up a cushion of slack.

Keep your casts short. All you need to do is flip your fly onto the water with the end of the rod. What could be easier?

Getting into proper position is important. Cast only from a spot where you can control the fly through the currents after it lands on the water. Don't expect the first cast to produce the perfect drift—these complex waters require a bit of experimentation. It may take several casts to find the spot that will take the fly through the pocket you want to fish. Charles Brooks, a master of fishing this kind of water, advised anglers to make at least ten casts to each pocket. From the proper position, casts are compact, and many can be made in a short time span.

Once you make a cast, use your rod to control the line. Your rod becomes nothing more than a long extension of your arm. The motions are more like fencing than fly fishing. Lift, drop, or twist your arm, thrust the rod like a rapier, or give a full-body lean to keep the fly line off the water. Your goal is to fish with only the leader and tippet, and perhaps a foot of line. You can adjust the float of the fly before it reaches the spot where you expect to find a trout. At this point, a bit of drag won't matter. It takes only a second or two of float to induce a strike. Once the fly is through the pocket, pick it up and cast again. A trout will rarely chase a fly from his home pocket.

Nymphs and wet flies are fished in much the same manner as dries. Make short casts, or use your rod to place nymphs in plunge pools, deep pockets, and around rocks. Using an indicator will help you watch the drift of the fly and ensure that it floats through a feeding lane. Once the fly is through your target pocket, lift it quickly from the water to avoid hanging up on the rocks below.

Cast to the front of a pocket, lift with the rod to keep the line off the water and the leader tight, and allow the fly to drift back into the pocket. While trout may not like to sit in areas of foam, you can cast to choppy water and drift a fly into a pocket below. You can also cast into the head of a plunge pool and let the current push the fly out from the foam and into the slack water.

A note of caution: Wading in pocket water can be dangerous. Deep pools, sudden drop-offs, and the rocky nature of the banks demand that you remain agile. I find bulky and heavy chest waders too cumbersome, so I wear hip boots in pocket water and wade as little as possible. Lighter waders allow me to remain highly mobile and make the quick movements necessary to maneuver around rocks and boulders. In summer, wet wading is a pleasant alternative. Small-stream pocket water can be fished from the banks, making wading unnecessary. For big and dangerous pocket water where wading is impossible, lug-soled hiking boots provide the best traction on slippery rocks along the banks.

Plucking trout from pocket water goes beyond mere fishing. It is a total adventure. Half the fun is getting to the water and boulder-hopping along the banks to work into position for a cast. The quickness with which a trout snatches a dry fly from the foaming surface ranks this among the most exciting types of fly fishing. The scenery is always magnificent. On a more intimate scale, the elegant patterns of water running over rocks are as beautiful as the trout that live there.

Chapter Six

Brushy-Stream Tactics

Fly fishing is by nature a solitary affair that is best practiced at times and in locations where anglers can have long stretches of stream to themselves. I tend to take this dictum to extremes and feel crowded when even a lone angler intrudes on my personal-space bubble—which extends at least a half mile in all directions. I used to think that my reasons for seeking utter solitude extended from embarrassment over my sloppy casting style to the risk of looking foolish when I couldn't scare up a trout. Gradually I discovered that it had nothing to do with my skills. Solitude is simply part of the total angling experience. On any given day on the water, my major goal is not to catch a mess of trout, but to totally immerse myself in the mountains. You can't do that when some guy named Buddy ambles up and asks the number one irrelevant question of angling: "Any luck?"

The most challenging part of fly fishing on a summer holiday weekend has little to do with trout—it has everything to do with finding solitude for the day's adventure. The easily accessible streams are bumper to bumper with fair-weather anglers bent on taking home a full limit. Streams that are a bit more hidden still have more than their share of anglers, or at least enough to burst a ridiculously large personal-space bubble. And surely there will be someone to ask that other silly angling question: "Whatcha usin'?"

So I've developed a small list of nearby "holiday streams," the places I'm certain to have to myself even on the busiest of weekends. Looking over the list, I've discovered they all have two things in common—each is a tiny stream, able to be crossed in a single bound, and each is brushy, with nearly every foot of the banks lined with willows, alders, and assorted other members of the plant kingdom.

Brushy streams are the orphans of the angling water— places that no one seems to want. And to be honest, there is good reason. Out of all the types of mountain water, brushy streams are the most frustrating to fly fish. It's not the good kind of frustration like you experience when you get to a challenging spring creek and find it loaded with bugs, with trout rising everywhere, but none will take your fly. It's the kind of frustration that makes you wonder why you are on the water at all, or, for that matter, why you ever took up fly fishing in the first place. It's the kind of frustration that is dangerous to the well-being of your fly rod.

It's impossible for even the most skilled anglers to fly fish a brushy stream without repeatedly snagging flies in the shrubbery. Because you must use the fly line and not some added weight to propel the flies, brushy streams never offer enough room to maneuver. Casting is difficult at best and is often impossible, and when you do find enough sky for an awkward cast, if the cast is not nearly perfect, the fly won't even hit the narrow ribbon of water.

Small, brushy streams come in an assortment like chocolates in a box. A few high-mountain waters are rocky and brush lined but are wide enough so that you can stand midstream and pop off a decent roll cast. These are fine places to start practicing the techniques required on the other, more diminutive waters. Tiny creeks—those that can be crossed by a single, long stride—hold trout, too. Most often the banks of these threads of water are a broken wall of vegetation, with plenty of overhanging branches to spice up the angling. Once when I needed a photograph of a brook trout, the most likely lie was located beneath a tunnel of willows. Never have I worked so hard for a 5-inch trout!

Why put yourself through such angling torture? Well, you're almost guaranteed to have the stream to yourself. But even if your desire for solitude doesn't border on the eccentric, brushy streams are worth taking a look at. When things go right and you manage to get your fly to drift a few feet on the surface, there is almost always a trout waiting to inhale it.

Reading Short Stories

Angling small streams forces you to make a few adjustments. It's a bull-in-a-china-shop situation: You can't bring large river attitudes and techniques to these delicate waters where subtlety counts more than brute force.

The first mental dial you have to turn is that of expectation. Small streams hold small fish, although there may be plenty of them. There isn't enough food to support monster trout, and, more importantly, prime holding water is often lacking. The fish simply don't get the chance to grow quickly like their cousins in more voluminous waters. My favorite brushy creek is the Rito de los Frijoles in Bandelier National Monument. I know spots here where if you step into the water, dozens of 5-inch rainbows will scatter off in every direction, bouncing off your feet in their hurry to escape. When I head to the Frijoles, I expect to catch a couple dozen rainbows less than 7 inches and a couple of 9-inch brook trout— veritable prizes in a stream that is never wider than one section of my two-piece rod. The Frijoles offers pounds of fun rather than pounds of fish flesh.

The cramped quarters of small streams also require you to modify your tackle a bit. It might seem that small water would go best with a small rod—and I've seen 6½-foot sticks in such water—but your standard 8½-foot rod will do just fine. A couple of changes in your terminal tackle will compensate. Tie on a short leader that is no more than 6 feet long. Anything longer will wind up in the trees. Use a foot of fairly stout tippet, no less than 5X, because you will snag leaves often and lighter tippet will frequently snap as you try to free the line.

Waders are useless on most creeks because you hardly spend any time in the water, and when you do, it's only ankle deep. You can wear a pair of running shoes if you like to get wet, but I find that the hiking boots that got me to the stream in the first place work best. You need some protection for your feet while fighting through the brush, and boots fit that bill, too. Waterproof boots also allow you to cross the stream or step into shallow water as necessary without getting your socks soaked. Long pants are also a help when fighting through the thorny shrubs, the poison ivy, and the stinging nettle that are usually found in canyon bottoms.

Unlike open or mid-sized streams, you won't fish every inch of brushy creeks. As you pick and choose the spots to concentrate your efforts, you'll cover a lot of ground—maybe as many as two miles in a morning. Skip over the unproductive water and the plentiful locations where it doesn't seem worth the effort to wrestle with the greenery to get a fly on the water. Concentrate on the biggest of the pools and places that have some casting potential. You can work upstream on relatively open stretches of water, but for the most brush-covered reaches, heading downstream is more effective. No matter which direction you go, avoid spooking fish unnecessarily by moving slowly with caution and care.

Reading the water of a small stream is like reading a short story rather than a novel. It only takes a few glances to get the full message. Many stretches of tiny streams are shallow—only ankle deep. You won't find many trout willing to brave the dangers of such water for a few insects. Instead, the smaller fish are concentrated around and under rocks and in small riffles that break up the shallow sections. If you're looking for the best fish in tiny water, seek out the pools. Watch for those rare spots where the water is maybe a foot deep. Find the spots where rocks, or more often logs, form natural dams. Upstream you'll find some slack water that is hard to reach, but it will be worth the effort in terms of the trout that patrol there. Downstream from the dams are dinner-plate pools that usually hold the relative lunkers. On very brushy streams where the flow is often hidden from view, use your ears to locate the dams and falls below them.

On the warmest afternoon of this past mountain summer, I spent the day on the Rito de los Frijoles. My guess was that bright sun, a blanket of heavy air, and midday timing would conspire to force the tiny brookies and rainbows into whatever disappearing act they could perform. Tall Douglas firs shaded the creek from high above, and alders, willows, and oaks lurked just above shoulder level. With little direct sun on the water, the trout fed freely throughout the afternoon while I did an hour of experimenting. As soon as I hooked a fish, I changed flies. In the course of the test, a size 14 Adams, a size 8 Joe's Hopper, three colors of Woolly Worm, a Partridge and Green soft hackle, and a foam beetle imitation took fish. The lesson was that even when conditions seem inappropriate for fly fishing, brushy-stream trout will take anything that floats by.

Over the River and through the Woods

The one essential rule to successful fly fishing on brushy streams hasn't a thing to do with trout. If you want a relatively hassle-free day of angling, you simply must control your fly line and leader at all times. Maintaining control is just as important when you aren't angling as when you are. If your line is free to swing when you are just moving upstream or downstream, your leader or your fly will snag a leaf as surely as a trout has spots.

Secure your line and leader to your rod whenever you are moving through the brush. When you are walking a few minutes to another location, use the fly loop provided on most rods. You'll lose a lot of fishing time if you reel in the fly and hook it to the loop when you are moving only a few feet from one casting location to another. But even when you're moving a couple of feet, it's a good idea to use your free hand to grab the tippet at the fly and pull the line taut. Pinch the line against the rod with the index finger of your rod hand, then drape the leader under the same finger and hold it secure. You should have less than a foot of tippet between your rod and your free hand.

When you are moving through the brush, it's often best not to hold your rod straight up and down. Keep it parallel to the ground at a level that is above the underbrush and below the tree limbs. Moving among the trees in this way is a bit like threading a needle, but it will reduce the number of snags with which you must fight.

Once you've made a cast, retrieving the fly back through the bushes can be a frustrating task. It's often best to back the rod away from the stream, parallel to the ground, by pulling it straight toward you. Once you're in the clear, raise the rod tip up and swing the fly to your hand. Sometimes it's easiest to just reel the fly all the way into the topmost guide on your rod.

When it's time for angling, the same rule applies—always control your line. The best way to do this is to limit your number of casts and to keep rod movement at a minimum. Make every cast count, and don't waste casts on unproductive locations. Don't bother with false casting—it's an invitation to hang up in the trees. Keep your casting distances short—less than 15 or even 10 feet—and you'll stand a better chance against snagging. Short leaders and tippets will help, and keeping all but a few inches or a foot of fly line off the end of the rod will ease the burden in most situations.

No matter what you do and how cautious you are, you'll get hung up. It's a matter of how often you can stand plucking snagged flies from the bushes or unwrapping a leader wound like a cocoon around a toothpick branch. When it stops being fun, pack up and go.

ROLLING ALONG

Not every creek is so small or brushy that you have no room to maneuver. Many headwater streams are wide enough to allow you to walk up the middle or work from one bank. On these waters, the banks are a wall of vegetation, but overhanging branches are not a problem. On these creeks you can get off a good cast if you constantly scout out both the forward cast and the backcast. On brush-lined streams where you can work roll and sideways casts, fish upstream.

On most small, brushy streams, however, you will almost never have any room to make a backcast. When your backcast is limited by trees or shrubs, a roll cast can send your line out the necessary distance. The trick of the roll cast is to send a loop of line from the rod tip to the water, much like the action you use to unsnag a rope or a garden hose that is hung up on some obstacle and you're too lazy to walk over and remove it. The roll cast starts with a stationary rod and is executed with a firm chopping motion.

To start the cast, bring your rod tip up until it points to the zenith. Wait a couple of seconds for the line to drift slightly behind the rod so that it is draped directly from the rod tip to the water. With a quick downward movement of a stiff arm, send the line straight out. It takes less force to do this than most anglers apply, and as a result, many find the leader piled up at the end of the cast. If this happens during your roll cast, ease up on the force. Don't end the downward motion parallel to the stream. Rather, stop the rod at about a 30-degree angle from the surface. With the proper force, you should be able to get off a 20-foot cast—usually all you need on small waters.

More useful and easier to pull off is the sideways cast. This is employed when you are working along one bank of a brushy stream where overhanging tree branches would snare a normally cast fly. It's a standard cast done perpendicular to its normal position. Instead of pointing the rod straight up, your arm and the rod move sideways. Stand facing the opposite bank and bring your rod down parallel to the surface of the water, pointing toward the opposite bank. You can make a short false cast by swinging the rod between the 10 o'clock and 2 o'clock positions of the now-horizontal clock. The rod will be moving just above the surface of the water and the fly will stay under the trees. With this cast you can work out 20 or 25 feet of line without much effort.

In some situations, a sidearm roll cast will be the perfect cast to avoid the trees. Roll casts are much easier to execute when, instead of holding the rod straight up, you begin with it pointing toward the opposite bank. Use the same basic technique—hold the rod still, parallel to the surface, and wait for the line to drift slightly behind the rod tip. A quick, stiff-arm motion will propel the fly toward the target. From this position, the line is much less likely to bunch up at the end of the cast.

Casting without Loading the Rod

Over the years, I've fished about five miles of the Rito de los Frijoles and found only three places where anything that resembles a standard cast will work. There are just too many bushes, and the stream is too small. Under such conditions, the goal is simply to get the fly on the water, then work it with the rod tip to set up a proper float. Fishing the Frijoles requires dapping, bow casts, wind casts, and the weighted-fly swing method, none of which require loading the rod in the traditional sense. These unorthodox techniques have added up to many afternoons of fun.

Keep in mind that on these streams your main goal is to get a fly on the water. If you succeed by any means, your fly should get a look from a trout. You want to play a fly—wet or dry, upstream or downstream—through each of the likely spots. How you do it is something else again.

The most basic method for angling brushy small streams is to use the rod just like a boy's cane pole and plop a fly directly on the water. It's not quite the same technique as traditional English dapping—holding a stiff rod above a lake and allowing the wind to dance the fly across the surface—but it usually goes by the same name.

Keeping your arm straight, ease the rod tip through the bushes and out over the water. Strip only enough line off the reel to have the leader and, at most, a couple feet of fly line extending down from the rod tip. Simply dangle the fly off the end of the rod and set it straight down onto the water. Once the fly is on the surface, you have three choices on how to fish your "cast." You can either fish a short dead drift over a suspected lie, hold the rod rigid and let the current bounce the fly up and down in the same spot, or lightly shake the rod to dance the fly on the surface. Control the movement of the fly by raising or lowering the rod tip a few inches. If you keep the rod high and the line taut, the fly will dance over the same riffle. If you lower the rod tip slowly as soon as the fly hits the surface, you can get more of a float before the dance begins. One caution—watch out for spider webs that can snag your fly and interrupt your dapping.

Dapping a fly is one way of fighting brush on small streams.

Dapping works best with bushy flies that catch a lot of air or water movement. Wulff-series flies fit the bill, as do Humpys and Irresistibles. You don't want to go too big or too small for your flies. A size 10 is by far too much for small water, and anything size 16 or less won't stand up to the wind or current very effectively. When dapping, I suggest you use size 12 or 14 patterns.

Of course, standing close to the stream directly over a pool or run puts the dapping angler pretty much in view of any trout beneath the surface. Concealment is the rub in the dapping process. So make use of that which forces you to use the method in the first place—the thick vegetation. Screen your body from view of the trout with a shoulder-high shrub. I wouldn't want to eliminate the possibility of crouching behind a low bush or even lying down a few feet back from the bank. Sometimes you can use foam from a plunge in the current to shield yourself from view. Be creative in your use of the environment to work in closer to your target.

Normally, fly fishers consider the wind an enemy, but on brushy streams you can use a variation of dapping to put the wind to work as an ally. If the wind is blowing in the direction in which you want your fly to go, casting won't be necessary. Get your rod tip and fly line out over the water. Hold the rod as high as it will go without hitting the trees, and allow the wind to catch the fly and blow it upstream or downstream. When it reaches maximum extension, drop the rod and the fly will follow, alighting on the surface some distance from your position. Then fish the drift like you would any other cast.

If you are using nymphs, wet flies, or streamers—any weighted flies—use the swing or pendulum cast to get the fly near your target. This technique takes advantage of what little weight the fly gives to the end of the line. Holding your arm stiff and high to get the rod over any greenery that lies between you and the stream, swing the rod in the direction away from your target. The weighted fly will pull the fly line. At the end of the backward motion of the fly, rock your arm forward and allow the fly to swing like a pendulum toward your target. In this manner, you can hit the head of a small pool or the start of a short run that might hold a trout.

Stiff rod techniques are effective in maybe half of the decent stretches of a brushy stream. When I can't work in close to the water, or the banks offer sparse protection, I resort to my favorite little trick—the bow cast. Rather than depend on wind or weight to get the fly onto the water, the bow cast loads the upper few feet of the rod and snaps the fly toward the target. The rod acts like an archer's bow to load and release the line. There's a limit to how far the cast will go, because it's not easy to use the bow cast to shoot line out of the guides. In fact, this method is only good for casts of 6 to 15

Bow Cast

To execute a simple bow cast, have about 2 feet of fly line extending from the rod tip. 1) Take the fly in your nonrod hand and pull the line taut. 2) Hold your arm straight out from your body and point your rod toward the target. Gently pull back on the fly and bend the rod tip slightly. 3) Let go of the fly. The bent rod tip will snap back straight, pulling the fly along with it.

Small streams don't necessarily mean small trout, as the cutthroat on the end of this line demonstrates.

feet. Despite its limitations, the bow cast can deliver the fly through narrow gaps in the greenery.

To execute a simple bow cast, take line off the reel that is about 2 feet longer than the length of the rod. Take the fly in your nonrod hand and pinch it firmly upside down so that the hook point is away from your fingers. Use the index finger of your rod hand to clasp the line running through the guides against the rod. Hold your arm straight out from your body and point it toward the target. Carefully pull back on the fly, which, in turn, will bend the rod tip. You only need to pull back about 6 inches and flex the tip. You don't need to warp it into a quarter-circle. Aim the rod toward your target and get ready to release the fly. Make certain that your head and ear are out of the firing line of the fly and that your fingers are clasping the fly behind the hook point. When all is ready, let go of the fly. The bent rod tip will snap back straight, pulling the fly along with it. The short bit of line will straighten, too, propelling the fly to the water.

The bow cast permits you the relative luxury of being able to launch a fly a few feet upstream or downstream. Because there is some force behind the cast—not like the dangling, at-the-mercy-of-the-wind method of dapping—you can shoot the fly through openings in the brush. You can stand or crouch back from the stream banks and worry a little less about being spotted by the trout. Use the bow cast to pop a fly into pools or up to the head of short runs. When the fly is on the water, fish the drift in the standard manner.

You can get a bit more distance out of your bow cast by coiling line in your hand before the cast. This will permit line to fly easily through the guides during the cast. Before you set up your bow cast, twist a few feet of fly line around your rod hand using the same finger-winding technique you would use for a hand-twist retrieve. When you make your cast, let go of the fly. A moment later, release the coil of line in your other hand. With practice, you can add up to 4 feet to your casts with this technique.

One more nontraditional method of angling will see you through the very brushy spots on small streams—let the current carry your fly to the target by fishing downstream floats. Angling with the current will let you reach the otherwise impossible lies, like those under a tunnel of vegetation or spots where dapping or even a bow cast would risk putting the fish down. Downstream floats work best with streamers and wet flies, but carefully controlled dry flies can also be used with confidence.

To use the downstream float, position yourself upstream from a good pool or run that is protected by overhanging branches. Don't work too close to the pool, but crouch at a point 15 or 20 feet above the best lie. If there's enough cover, you can stand in or straddle the stream, but most of the time

Fish downstream to put a fly under a tunnel of vegetation.

you'll want to work from the bank. Use whatever method is appropriate to get the fly on the water—a bow cast or a swing usually does it. Move the rod tip to get your fly in the proper float line, then strip a few feet of line off the reel and feed it downstream at the same speed the current moves. You may have to shake the rod tip back and forth gently to force the line through the guides. If the fly is still a few feet from the target, you can readjust the float with the rod tip—an easy upstream pull usually won't spook the fish. Keep the line moving at the proper speed through the target area and be prepared to strike.

It is important to watch out for the direction of the strike when you are fishing downstream. When a fish rises for the fly, you run the risk of pulling the imitation from its mouth if you strike too quickly. When you are fishing upstream, the strike serves to pull the fly into the fish's mouth. The secret here is to hesitate a moment between the rise and the strike. When you see the flash of a trout, wait long enough to take a quick breath before you pull back ever so slightly on the rod tip. Hopefully, you've given the trout the opportunity to turn with the fly in its mouth, and your tug will be just enough to set the hook. If you pull the fly before the trout grabs it, the fish might give chase. If you miss the hook-up, quickly make another cast. Chances are the trout will at least take another look.

I'll admit that even the solitude of the Rito de los Frijoles isn't enough to get me to carry my rod down into its canyon more than once a year. Even so, at some point in the middle of the trip, I'm bound to mumble in disgust, "This is nuts." But before long those little trout, shining in the sunlight, and the simplistic angling methods required to take them, turn my attitude around. When I strike poorly and miss an 8-inch brookie and hear myself moan out loud, "Oow. Good fish!" I know I'm singing the song of the brushy stream.

CHAPTER SEVEN

The Beauty of Meadow Water

Following the long-established pattern, I emerged from the cocoon of the tent, leaving my wife and kids undisturbed. As the halo over the peaks to the east swelled, I made coffee and grabbed a muffin, using them to keep me from dashing off too early to the stream that whispered the only sounds that breezed through the pines. I rigged a fly rod, then slid out of the shade of the forest into the glaring sunlight that filled the meadow below. It was still way too early for trout to find enough bugs on the water to have them in a feeding frenzy, but that wasn't the goal of this morning's angling. Like so many other times, I just wanted to be in that meadow as the shadows shrank from the stream up the valley walls. Being on the water gave me an excuse to linger along the water, where in the morning sun the splashes above the current danced like fairies in a Mendelssohn scherzo.

To some, meadows are the most exquisite places of beauty in a landscape that supplies more than enough superlatives. The meadows that line the streams in the highest county are a world unto themselves. Patches of snow linger deep into summer, lining the base of bare rock cliffs like chalk scribbles. The bold thread of the stream is woven into the texture

The slow-moving meanders of meadow water make for highly scenic and challenging fly fishing.

of the green grasses. Wildflowers dot the ground like colored raindrops.

The beauty of meadows derives not only from the scenery, but also from the angling. With wide-open spaces, casting is generally snag-free, although a low backcast will frequently find a tuft of grass or the brilliant head of a sunflower. The water is usually calm, which makes for more relaxed angling. Depending on where you choose to spend your time, you can have some of the easiest angling found anywhere, or you can let yourself in for some demanding hours where all your angling skills come into play.

The Gibbon River in Yellowstone National Park is a perfect example of both types of meadow water. A few miles below its headwaters in Grebe Lake, the tiny stream snakes through a long meadow. The river, hidden by swaying grasses, is only five steps wide and is usually less deep than a decent trout is long. Brook trout, most of them no bigger than 10 inches, freely rise throughout the meadow any time of day. My ten-year-old daughter and I spent an hour there one cloudy summer day, and it was the first time she told me, "I can do this myself, Dad." And she could. I headed downstream, and it wasn't long before I heard her shouts of delight as she reeled in more than a couple of nice brookies. In fact, she outfished me by a long shot.

The tables were turned later that day only 12 miles downstream. We stopped at Elk Park, where the Gibbon flows through another meadow, but now the river was much wider and deeper and was filled with educated browns and rainbows longer than my daughter's arm. The slow turns of the river reflected the forested peaks to the west as clearly as any lake surface. My daughter couldn't get away with any mistakes, and she knew it. She folded quickly. Armed with a bit more skill and patience, I stuck with it for an hour and was rewarded with one brown—the type measured in pounds, not inches.

The wide-open spaces of meadows are usually formed on the flat floors of glacial valleys or on the level beds of long-vanished lakes. The character of headwater streams rushing out from the peaks like runaway locomotives is suddenly and completely changed. From straight-line strings of cascades, the streams take a breather and lazily meander across the fields through sweeping turns in a hypnotic rhythm. In some places, the flow is so arrested that the rivers look more like stretched out lakes than flowing water.

The low-gradient, flat water—combined with the broad turns—can create healthy trout habitat. The flow can deepen or it can spread out, each alternative creating a different style of fishing that will appeal to opposite types of anglers. Where the flow spreads and the water becomes shallow, the lack of protection combines with consistent food sources to produce a fishery with lots of small trout that willingly take anything that floats by. Such meadow water is made to order for beginners and kids. When the flow slows and deepens, languishing currents, perfectly transparent water, and the presence of deep undercuts in the wide turns can yield big, finicky trout that are difficult to fool.

Clear Water and Spooky Trout

The shallow meanders of meadows are often overlooked by anglers, and that's why I take my kids to these spots. They learned to fly fish in calf-deep streams flowing through grasslands. From New Mexico to Montana, I can picture beetle-green meadows within 2 or 3 miles of the road where we've pitched our tent and spent a couple of days on the water. The lack of streamside vegetation makes casting a bit easier than in most mountain locations, where backcasts are usually cramped. The shallow water and silty bottoms make it easy for the kids to wade in sandals, and I don't have to worry about deep holes or fast currents giving them a dangerous spill. Most important is the number of fish, usually brookies, that make it a snap for the kids to spot a riser or to find a hidden trout in a likely spot against the bank. The fish don't mind the fluffy white wings of a House and Lot, and when the kids can see the fly on the calm water, they have a chance to at least see the strike. These are places that turn kids into fly fishers because it is so easy to succeed.

For experienced anglers, shallow waters in small meadows make for some easy pickin's. At the high elevations of most headwater streams there aren't a lot of nutrients in the stream and insects aren't abundant. Trout are always on the lookout for food floating by and will eagerly take flies. The only difficulty in fishing such waters is finding the fish, and even this is like reading a children's book. Spot the places that are a bit deeper than the rest of the stream. Most often you'll find nice runs along the banks where the river bends. Logs or tree-root obstructions will back up small pools. Where the flow drops over a gravel bar, you'll usually find a pocket of smooth water deep enough for nice trout. Look, too, at the base of plunges and behind the few rocks that may be scattered throughout the flow. Once you've found the target of deeper water, pop a dry fly to it and get ready for the strike. It's the most basic kind of fly fishing you'll find anywhere.

The paradox of meadows is that, depending on their characteristics, they can be the easiest or among the most difficult places to fly fish. Those extremes can be found even within the same half-mile meadow run. For our last overnighter of the year, we did a daddy-daughter trip with some friends. The girls were anxious to catch a few trout, so I chose a meadow in the San Juan Mountains that holds a decent population of little brook trout. The daughters fished the upper portion of the meadow where the brookies reside in a shallow, rippling stream with undercuts. Their unrefined casts were enough to snare a few trout each. Two hundred yards downstream, the dads were getting an education from the much larger rainbows that worked the broad meanders where the creek deepened to 6 or 7 feet. The surface was so still you couldn't tell there was a current. A dozen trout rose to take invisible insects, but they proved to be as cautious as a new father with his baby. The most delicate presentations of tiny or monster flies left them unmoved.

Deep, slow-moving meadow water is the most challenging of the mountain-water situations. I'll usually walk right by the toughest spots and head to some pocket water. I reserve meadows for times when I have the luxury of puzzling through the perfect presentation and the opportunity to try every fly in my box. When the time is right, I follow mountain-water rules and try to keep the angling as simple as possible.

I don't think you have to worry about meadow fish being leader shy, but they will be line shy. So you want to put a little

To keep a low profile when angling in open meadows, cast from the kneeling position.

distance between your fly line and your fly. Use a leader that's a little longer than one you would normally use on a small stream. Make your leader between 7 and 9 feet long.

Meadows don't offer much protection for a trout, so chances are there will be one in every lie. To fish a meadow effectively, cast to even the smallest protected spaces. Look for deep currents along the banks, small pockets squeezed between two overhanging branches, and even the scalloped half-circles that are eroded out of the bank. Most casts on a meadow stream will be straight upstream or slightly to one side. Put your fly very close to where a fish lies.

You need to exhibit a bit more care on meadow waters than you would on, say, a riffle or slick on the same river farther downstream. With the smooth, glassy surface of slow meanders, the trout's visual field is expanded. You need to keep not only yourself but your rod and line hidden from view. Manufacturers make waders with reinforced knees specifically with this type of low-profile, stealth angling in mind. On open water, bend down on your approach to the water and cast from a crouch or on your knees. Always head upstream, but when you are just walking and not working into position for a cast, walk far back from the banks. Stepping right along the stream will scatter the fish in that reach, and they will alarm the others upstream where you are heading.

Many anglers aren't aware of how their rod and line over the water affect the trout below. The flash of a whipping rod, the curl of a fly line, or the glint of sun off a rod guide will put the fish onto you and have them on their guard. You have to keep all that motion over the water to a bare minimum. Cut down on false casting and make your real casts count. Avoid disturbing the surface or the air above the water any more than is absolutely necessary. It's a good idea to false cast *away* from the direction of your target, off to the side and well behind where you want to place your cast. This will eliminate the rod and line moving over the water and will shake off the excess water on the fly line onto the grass and not onto the calm water where you are stalking trout.

When you come across a glassy stretch of water where trout are feeding on delicate mayflies, you'll have to resort to the parachute cast to gently ease your fly to the water. When used in conjunction with parachute-style fly patterns, this casting technique will put your imitation on the water without rippling the surface and making the fish suspicious.

The trick to a parachute cast is to have out more fly line than you need to reach the target with a straight-line cast. With an extra couple of feet of line, begin by making a standard cast. A moment before your arm reaches the end of its forward motion, stop. Drop the butt end of the rod downward. The fly line will spring slightly back on itself, forming

Narrow headwater streams are often deeper than they are wide.

random curves in the line. Then slowly drop the rod tip and the swerving line will float gently to the surface.

Fly fishers always picture the line from a cast as heading out over and landing on the water, but it doesn't have to be that way. One method that gives you a decided advantage in meadow waters is the cross-country cast. Instead of sending line out over water, you cast so that the fly line lands on the ground and only the leader and tippet land on the water. Use this technique when you want to keep surface disturbance by your line at a minimum, when you are casting to bank feeders, or when you don't want to reveal any profile to the trout in the stream.

When you are heading upstream in open country, you'll often spot what looks to be a decent trout feeding in a quiet pool ahead. With nothing to use as cover, you will alert the trout to your presence and send it packing no matter what approach you use. Don't panic. Move away from the stream on the side

CROSS-COUNTRY CAST

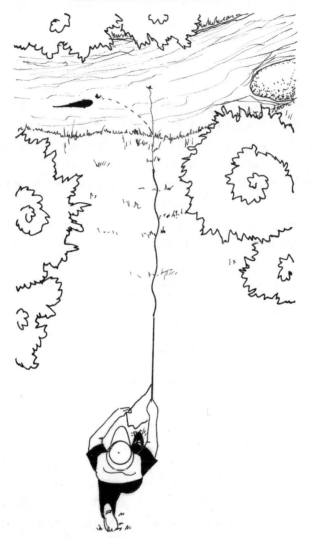

To make a cross-country cast, stay well back from the bank—at least 20 feet. Kneeling helps to keep you out of sight of the trout. Strip enough line from your reel to put your fly just over the bank. With as little false casting as possible, cast your line perpendicular to the stream bank. When you cast, have all the fly line and the first bit of leader fall on the grass. The fly will hit the water and swing a few feet downstream.

where the trout is feeding. Head back 50 feet, then move in the direction of the trout, staying well back from the bank. When you come opposite to the fish, crouch down and move in a bit closer so that your cast will be only 25 feet or so. Strip off enough line to get your fly just over the bank. With as little false casting as possible—and making sure that each false cast is short and not over the water—cast your line perpendicular to the stream bank. The goal is to have the line and the first bit of leader fall on the grass, with only a few feet at the end of the leader landing on the water at the spot where the fish is feeding. This method takes a little practice, because you have to be able to judge the distance without mistakenly putting the line over the water. Going a bit short is better, but if the fly lands on the grass, it has a nasty habit of snagging there.

The perpendicular cross-country cast is also effective for getting a fly to bank feeders that can't be reached from the opposite bank. It's also fun to fish this cast blind, putting a fly along the bank where the grass is high and you can't see where the fly lands on the water. You don't have to see the fly to make an accurate strike. Listen carefully for the sound of a gulp or the splash of the rise, or you can watch the leader where it drapes over the grass. Any sudden movement is likely a fish on your fly.

It's more of a challenge to pull off a cross-country cast that runs parallel to the stream. You can accomplish this with a variation of the simple reach cast, and it can get you into a decent fish when nothing else will work. When you find a trout feeding along the bank just downstream from a willow that reaches into the water, the situation is ripe for an upstream cross-country cast. Because you can't approach the fish from upstream or to the side, your only chance is to cast from directly downstream. If you put the leader over the fish, it'll most likely turn tail and hide. Try this maneuver: Make a

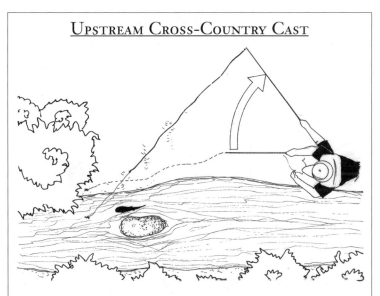

UPSTREAM CROSS-COUNTRY CAST

Use the upstream cross-country cast, a variation of the reach cast, to place a fly in difficult spots where you want to keep the leader from floating over a fish. 1) Make a cast directly upstream directly along the bank. 2) As the line straightens out, reach with your casting arm away from the stream. Allow the line to fall on the grass, with the leader and fly falling on the water.

cast directly upstream directly along the bank. As the line straightens out, reach with your casting arm away from the stream and let the line settle. The line will fall on the grass, but the last-second reach will put a curve in the end of the line and will keep the leader and fly over the water. If you do this correctly, the fly will land upstream from the fish, with the leader off to the side, and you'll get a brief drift over the trout, which is usually enough.

Where the grasses are tall or low shrubs line the banks, you can get away with an approach to the stream very close to where a fish lies. In this situation, you don't have to cast at all. Here you can try dapping a fly blindly over the grass and onto the water along the bank. Hold the rod high, but try and keep all but the tip behind the bank. You can drop your fly onto the surface and guess how your fly is floating along, or you can dance the fly on and just above the surface in hopes of inducing a strike. Listen carefully for the sound of the take, then lift the rod tip gently to set the hook.

TERRESTRIALS AND MOUNTAIN TROUT

All of the major groups of aquatic insects are found in meadow streams. Mayflies produce thin hatches, usually in midmorning and early evening, and caddis flies are mainly afternoon and evening fliers. Even the small stoneflies—yellow and green sallies—get into the act and can produce light hatches in the high country. However, the meadow streams lack the thick hatches that dominate rivers at lower elevations. In the absence of abundant aquatic insects in mountain water, terrestrials play a dominant role in the diet of trout. High-country meadows always demand a fly box well-stocked with beetles, ants, and hoppers.

My kids are like most others who haven't yet become teens, I suspect, and they are rather indifferent to mealtime. They eat just enough to keep their energy levels up but rarely show any enthusiasm at dinnertime. The exception comes when the cycle rolls around to Saturday and it's pizza night. Suddenly, they'll even help set the table in anticipation. They dive at the pizza pan, wolf down the first piece, then head back for more.

The kids remind me of trout during grasshopper time.

When the languid days of midsummer reach the mountains in August, the trout have been lazily feeding on thin evening hatches for a month or so. They seem to have lost their gusto, and luring a fat brown or rainbow out of hiding with a mayfly pattern is increasingly difficult. When you are working a meadow stream, you'll think that the trout have all packed up and moved upstream to cooler waters. That is, until you hear the clicking buzz of a grasshopper, see its drunken flight smack into the water, and watch it immediately disappear with a splashing rise of a brown trout.

Hopper time is the most exciting time to be on meadow water. It seems that all species of trout—but particularly browns and rainbows—are very fond of grasshoppers. I think it's the pizza factor—a huge, filling, special treat that rewards the eater with lots of high-energy food for a minimum of effort. It seems that, to a trout, the taste of a hopper works like the magic of Turkish Delight—eat one and it gets kind of anxious to have more. Trout will rush from the protection of their lies, even through a couple vertical feet of water, to take a hopper with abandon. The instinct of hopper feeding overrides good sense in trout, and they will often take a hopper when nothing else works. In fact, on more than several occasions on tailwaters, I've forsaken the prevailing wisdom of small nymphs and fished huge hoppers with great success.

Young hoppers are found in the grasses surrounding meadow streams from June on, but it isn't until they grow big and get the mating urge that they become important to anglers. From the first days of August to the heavy frosts of late October, hoppers can be found buzzing overhead and through the grasses, and falling on the water. They don't hatch like aquatic insects, but similarly, they are found on the water for a specific period each day. About the time you get hungry for lunch, maybe around 11 A.M., the hoppers get active and stay active until the sun starts heading toward the horizon—around 4 or 5 P.M.

Hoppers don't intentionally enter the water—no food or mates are to be found on the stream. Their clumsy, erratic style of flight sometimes leads them over the water and thus onto the surface. They seem to need no help in having a watery accident, but a bit of wind can create havoc in the hopper world and send astonishing numbers of them into the water. Once on the water, hoppers kick with their grotesque hind legs and head for the banks, but if the currents are swift and choppy, they won't reach their goal and will eventually drown.

All this means fantastic angling opportunities for fly fishers. Hitting a meadow stream on a slightly cloudy and windy day can produce plenty of action. Trout will rush from nowhere to take your fly, and even if they miss, chances are your heart will take a moment to stop pounding its presto rhythm against your chest.

Most hopper patterns come with fat bodies, bushy legs, and apostrophes. On rippling meadow water, I don't think it matters at all if you like Dave's, Joe's, or Ralph's versions of the hopper. Pick one that you enjoy tying, and vary its size and color. Grab a few mountain hoppers and look at their bellies. You'll find yellow, but a few sport orange or green undersides, so you might want to carry a couple of colors. (Is a Joe's Hopper with a green body still a Joe's? I don't know, and I don't think it makes much difference.) Because trout seem to key on the color of hoppers, being prepared with some extras is worthwhile. Size depends on where the meadow is located. On big-meadow streams at lower elevations, you might see an occasional hopper that tapes out to size 6. In general, though, you'll want to use size 8 to 12 hoppers on big rivers. Grasshoppers in headwater meadows run smaller in the range of size 10 to size 14.

Consider the type of water you're fishing. High-floating, bushy, colorful patterns—like Joe's Hopper—are the ideal choice for the faster, more broken sections of meadow water. That flash of high-riding color is all you need to fool a trout. You want to keep the fly floating, and all that hackle works best. Flies with deer-hair bodies are also good floaters, and a Dave's Hopper is a classic that works best on fast-moving currents along the banks. When you are casting on smooth water, however, select a fly that rides lower on the surface. I'll usually pull out a Schroeder's Parachute Hopper in this situation. The horizontal hackle lets the fly sit right in the surface film, just like the real thing. The fly has an accurate silhouette and subdued colors and is thus more suitable for long looks from trout.

When fishing hoppers, it pays to be a bit of a sloppy caster. Hoppers usually hit the water with a splash, attracting the attention of trout. You want to do the same with your pattern, in both riffly and calm water. It doesn't take a snap of the wrist or a quick arm movement, but a bit of overpowering with your cast will send the hopper slamming into the surface. The splash won't work as well in choppy currents, but on smooth water, the splash will send out rings and announce to the fish that something big just landed. This is just what you want. If your pattern is drifting along on quiet water and not attracting any attention, twitch the rod tip to put a little kick in your pattern's legs. The twitch will send more ripples across the water and may be just enough to induce a take. The twitch method works great with hopper patterns with rubber legs, like a Madam X.

Another fun way to present your hopper is to cast the pattern onto the bank and yank it off onto the water with a plop. Cast slightly upstream from a bank-feeding trout or to a spot where you think you might find a good fish. Before the line starts to drag—and this means that you can't wait more than a couple of seconds—jerk the rod tip back a couple of inches and watch the fly jump onto the water. This is particularly effective where the current along the bank is strong and the surface is a bit broken.

Not being skilled swimmers, grasshoppers drown quickly in faster currents or choppy water; therefore, you can effectively fish hopper patterns wet or dry. When a pattern gets tired or sinks in the foam, fish out the cast as you would any dead-drifting wet fly. In rough water, you might have greater success if you start by fishing your hopper wet. A dead drift is all you need in this case.

Like grasshoppers, beetles come into play on meadow waters in mid- to late summer. These hard-shelled insects inhabit the meadow grasses and willows, but because they are less agile than hoppers, they don't get around as much. Beetles tend to fall into the water close to the bank, and feeding trout will sit inches from the bank below an overhanging patch of vegetation, watching for beetles floating downstream.

There are several easy ways to get beetle patterns to the bank feeders, but all involve stalking techniques. You need to keep the low profile required of all meadow fishing. If the stream is wide enough to permit you to work from the opposite side, you can simply use a quarter upstream cast to drift the pattern along the feeding lane. Cast as close to the bank as you can—sometimes 6 inches away is too far. You can also cast onto the bank and give a gentle tug to hop the pattern onto the water, but it's a little more difficult to come within a couple of inches of the bank that way. An effective place to drift a beetle is under an overhanging willow along the bank. Use a reach cast to put the fly below the rest of the fly line as it floats under the branches. If you can't work from the opposite bank, or if the stream is small and working in the water would expose you to the trout, try casting beetles along the banks using the cross-country cast.

Beetle patterns are designed to float low on the water, and this feature makes the flies difficult to see on the water. The most common solution to this problem is to put some type of fluorescent synthetic material on the beetle's back. The easiest beetle patterns to tie are black foam beetles with a strip of flashabou pulled over the back and perhaps a few strands left dangling to the sides like legs.

I hate to fish ant patterns—you can never see the things on the water. Drab colors—black or brown—and a low profile combine to make using ant patterns like fishing at night. But on smooth-surfaced meadow water, there are times when ants are the most effective pattern around. Clear afternoons come to mind. The aquatic insects are waiting for the clouds, and the wind is calm, meaning that hoppers and beetles won't be very effective. Casting ants can save such a day, if you are willing to give it the effort. I've found that the addition of a white wing post on my ant patterns takes away much of the pain of fishing ants. The post gives me something to see so that I have a chance of picking up the pattern on the water.

Chapter Eight

High-Country Stillwater

Midsummer days on the upper Rio Grande in the San Juan Mountains of Colorado is apt to make anyone feel like one of those 10 percent of the anglers who catch 90 percent of the fish. Around the evening's campfire, your ego-swollen rod gets too big for its case and your head too large for your hat. After such a day on the river, I planned the agenda for the next day—a hike up to a high-country lake hidden below the peaks. I needed an antidote in the form of a huge dose of reality. Two hours of climbing up the rocky trail brought me to a forest-rimmed lake that was bubbling with rising trout. Visions of 20-inch cutthroats danced in my head as I fumbled with the trappings of my rod and tackle. It seemed forever until I was rigged and making the first of 200 casts that followed, each of which had no payoff. In the presence of hundreds of feeding trout, I went fishless.

Stillwater fly fishing in the high country can be a humbling experience. The clear, quiet water gives most of the advantages back to the trout. They can take a long, lingering look at what you're trying to entice them with, your technique has to be refined enough to not scare away the fish, and there is little room for error.

High-country lakes are perhaps the most scenic of all mountain-angling destinations.

Lake and beaver-pond fishing can take on the characteristics of bait fishing, which is not my favorite way of spending time on the water. A lot of the techniques require patience, the ability to cast and wait, or simply to watch, wait, and cast at the right time. This kind of fishing lacks the constant searching, casting, and movement of stream fishing that has hooked me deeply. Much of the action is unseen as you cast a weighted pattern and scoot it along in the subsurface. There can be a lot of down time between casts. On some lakes you might as well give me a bobber and a beer.

Despite its shortcomings, lake fishing gives you the real opportunity to catch a decent-sized trout. My hours spent on the high lakes of New Mexico, Colorado, and Wyoming have taught me that with a few alterations, mountain-water rules still apply. It doesn't always take the perfect fly, a fine-tuned cast, or a lot of patience to catch the trout of your life.

After a seemingly endless 12-mile hike to base camp and a full 24 hours of eager anticipation, I made my first visit to an alpine lake. From camp, the 2,000-foot climb to the glacial bowl required huffing, but the view from the shores made the extreme shortness of breath bearable. What I saw of the lake, however, was confusing. Reared as I was on stream fishing, and accustomed as I was to reading the nuances of the water's surface to locate likely spots to toss a fly, the flat, featureless surface of a lake was daunting. Topside, every square foot of the lake seemed just like all the others—no telltale rings of rising trout broke the calm of the surface. Caddis flies bounced along, barely skimming the water in an erratic pattern, but they didn't seem to make an impression on whatever swam below. I couldn't get a fix on anything, didn't understand what was spread before me, and was quickly convinced that the lake was dead.

My fishing partner, savvy in the ways of high-country lakes, noted my confusion and quietly rigged his rod. While I sat taking in the scenery, he made his first casts. It only took three before his rod was pulled into an arc that could only mean big fish. I was in awe.

The mountain-water secret to lake fishing is the same as that for stream fishing. Trout hang out where they have some protection from predators and where food is in ample supply. In lakes, the best protection is afforded by the deep water that is usually beyond the limits of a fly caster standing on the shore. Your best bet is to look for structure, not on the surface but below it. Certainly there are plenty of trout plying the deeper waters of the lake, but you'll find a fair number utilizing the cover offered by rocks along the water's edge and just off shore.

One method that I learned quickly is to look at the geography and geology of the lake. Most high lakes were scoured

Casting to near-shore structure is the most effective way to fish an alpine lake.

by glaciers that were fed down from the surrounding peaks. Moving ice slices effectively through rocks, leaving behind steep walls of bare stone. At the foot of these walls lie fields of huge boulders collectively called talus. At any lake, I search for the talus, because that's where the near-shore subsurface structure is found. The talus slope extends from the foot of the cliff to the lake shore and continues below the surface of the water, providing the necessary cover for trout.

The other obvious choice on a lake is to concentrate your efforts at the inlet or outlet. There's usually a gang of fish hanging around the inlet, waiting for food to drift into the lake. It's a lot like stream fishing in still water. The surface is often rippling, affording you a bit of protection from being seen by the fish.

I've often considered dragging a float tube up to one of these high lakes, but the thought of loading up for the hike with another 15 pounds has always squashed the idea pretty quickly. I've regretted leaving the tube behind on only a couple of occasions when the only rising fish seemed to always linger 4 feet beyond my casting range. For the most part, however, you can adhere to the mountain-water rule of simplicity and not bother with the added aggravation of bringing along a tube. With most of the lake's structure and its inlet and outlet within reach of a cast made from the shore line or by wading in shallow water, reaching the middle of the lake is unnecessary. Yes, at times—when there's brush along the banks, the wind is blowing into shore, or walking on the rocks leaves you exposed to the fish—it would be nice to be able to cast inward toward the shore, but casting along the bank will usually accomplish your goal of putting a fly in sight of fish.

RISING TO THE OCCASION

Lake fishing is full of grand contrasts. Few sights are more exciting to the angler than the surface of a lake laced with intermingling rings pushed out by rising trout. And few times can be more frustrating than casting flies toward those rings, only to be rejected on all counts.

The timing of a good rise on a lake has much to do with the amount of sunlight on the water. Good rises can occur just after first light when the peaks are like a flat, paper cutout on the horizon. On cloudless days, the rise can continue until the sun touches the water. So it pays to be an early riser when you are camped at a lake. Grab a cup of coffee and a muffin and head for the water. Chances are, the rise will be over before the rest of the camp stirs. If possible, I like to start at the west end of a lake, then, as the sun rises, follow the shadow line east across the lake.

If you're the type who believes that getting up before the sun doesn't follow mountain water's simplification rule, be

Most of the structure in high-country lakes is near shore, and using a float tube is usually unnecessary.

cheered in the knowledge that the evening rise is usually more consistent. Fish as the sun drops to cast long shadows across the water.

During any trip to the high country, I'm always torn between my desires for sunny skies and cloudy afternoons. That rich blue sky makes hiking and camping more comfortable, but a bit of rain, or at least the threat of it, always brings better insect hatches and a longer, more consistent rise. Even in the high country, hatching insects can be stressed by the high, dry conditions that occur when the sun is shining. As a result, more bugs become adults on cloudy afternoons. When rain clouds have rolled in by noon, I've seen decent hatches begin by 2 P.M. and last until dusk. You can fool a lot of lake-dwelling trout in six hours!

One other weather factor can influence lake fishing and give a slight advantage to the angler. I find that a bit of wind helps me catch more fish. In the calm of the early morning, a lake surface is as smooth and reflective as a bathroom mirror. It's difficult to tell where lake ends and sky begins. You can follow the ripples radiated out from a rising trout for as much as 100 feet, and for the same reason it can be alarmed by the gentle plop of an improperly cast fly. Tippet and leader stand out on the water like a deep crack in a truck windshield. Fishing is tough.

But invariably as the night's cold air settles down from the warming peaks, a light breeze soon brushes across the lake and the surface becomes a mosaic of stillness and motion. The lightly dancing ripples in areas where the wind blows are great places to cast a fly. The glassy surface is broken by a breeze, the trout are not so wary, they don't get such a perfect view of your fly, and they aren't as likely to spot you on the bank. In short, they take flies more readily.

There are two basic techniques to fishing dry flies on lakes. The easiest is closely related to the stream-fishing techniques of searching out hidden fish. Just as you read the water of a stream and find likely lies behind rocks or along the banks, you can read the structure of lakes and cast there, hoping to lure a fish out of hiding. It's not as unlikely as it sounds. Most structure is easy to reach with a cast along the shoreline. There's usually a surprising assortment of bugs crawling around on the rocks or in the vegetation along the lake, and accidents do happen, even to insects. Wise trout line up at the base of rocks and wait for food to drop into the water. I can think of a couple of fish as long as my forearm that I've taken in only a foot of water by slamming a fly into a shoreline rock and having it drop onto the water an inch or two away from the base of the rock. So try your stream-angling techniques along the lakeshore. Cast to likely lies and let the fly sit there for a few seconds. If nothing happens, take a step and cast to the next lie.

Of course, it's much more fun to cast dry flies to rising trout. In clear water and in the right light, this technique can have its own unique challenge when you cast your fly and watch a 20-inch cutthroat swimming up toward it. The hard part is to not get too excited and pull the fly away before the fish grabs it!

A few fish in a lake will work a single spot, rising within a 1-foot radius time and time again. That's why I often wait for a rise, then pop my fly into the rings. It's not unusual to have the fish come up right away, but if it doesn't, let the fly sit for awhile before retrieving it. There's a chance another fish will come along and spot the fly.

Most fish work a circuit in the lake, cruising around slowly and watching for insects on the water. Some fish seem to work to a rhythm, and you can use this to fool them. Observe the lake surface for a few minutes and try to find a riser that seems to come up in a pattern or at a regular interval. If you can work out the rhythm, determine where the next rise will be and cast your fly there just before the next scheduled rise. It's a little more work than casting to a rise, but it sure is fun.

Sometimes the fish won't notice your fly right away. When you think you've given a trout enough time to see your pattern but nothing happens, it often helps to give the fly a twitch to attract attention. You don't want a whole lot of motion here—not a big jerk or a long pull, just a sudden half-inch slide. You're trying to mimic the natural motion of a caddis or maybe a mayfly and to send a few tiny ripples across the surface. Often this small movement is enough to trigger a response in the trout, and you'll get an immediate strike. If you don't, wait 5 or 10 seconds, then repeat the twitch. If four or five twitches don't produce a strike, then gently pull in the line and cast to another spot or to another rising fish.

It's best to use flies that you can see easily, but at the same time, remember that in a lake the trout can take a good look, too. In general, you want to use flies that are smaller and less gaudy than you would use on moving mountain water. Where you might select a size 10 or 12 imitation on a stream feeding into a lake, you want to go with a size 14 or maybe even a size 16 on a lake. Although white wings are great for making a fly visible in swift-moving water, you don't want that feature on a lake. More natural colors are the obvious choice, and more imitative patterns are often, but not always, more successful.

Parachute flies are always an excellent choice when mayflies are on the water, an occurrence that doesn't happen often on high lakes. Parachute flies permit you to make a more delicate presentation on a glassy lake surface. If there's one thing that will consistently put down stillwater trout, it's a splash from a supposedly near-weightless insect imitation. As an added advantage, the upright wing of a parachute pattern stands up enough to be readily visible from a distance. When you can't quite spot the fly on the surface, crouch down to get a line of sight right on top of the water. The post will be easy to spot.

The most common mayfly on high lakes in the Rockies is the speckle-winged *Callibaetis*. Hatches, which come from June through August, are generally thin, but the size 12 mayflies offer a juicy morsel to feeding trout. Emergence is quick, and trout will often ignore the midmorning hatch of *Callibaetis*. However, they won't refuse the spinner fall in the evening. I love to fish the spinner fall with a spinner pattern sporting wood duck–feather wings, but picking up the low-lying pattern presents a problem on long casts. Instead, I found that mountain-water rules often apply to the *Callibaetis* hatch and I use a Parachute Adams with better results.

In most clear, clean alpine lakes in the Rockies, surface feeding by trout is overwhelmingly on caddis and midges. On a still lake, you can watch the egg-laying caddis flies yo-yoing along an erratic line, dimpling the surface film ever so slightly every couple of feet. My lake fly box is filled with Elk Hair Caddis—the easiest caddis pattern to tie—in sizes 12 to 18 with gray, yellow, green, brown, and orange bodies. I throw in some tiny midge dries, some flying ants, and a few beetle patterns because, more than anything else, they look nice.

But I've got to tell you, the fly that has brought me more lake trout during the evening rise breaks all the accepted norms—except, of course, mountain-water rules. The fly is aptly named—the Renegade. Here's a simple fore-and-aft-hackled imitation that is as impressionistic as they get. It's the type of fly that shouldn't work on a lake where a long inspection by a trout usually results in his ignoring the offering. It's generally thought that the contrasting white and brown hackles of the Renegade look like the fluttering wings of a caddis fly. I'm not going to argue with that interpretation. I once fished a single Renegade on a Wyoming lake to the tune of more than a dozen 3- to 4-pound brook and cutthroat trout in the space of one remarkable hour.

The secret of the Renegade's success is adding that little twitch to the motionless pattern sitting quietly on the water. A half-inch of pull on the rod tip will cause the Renegade to jump a bit on the surface. With the fluttering-wing look, the motion seems to trigger a now-or-never reflex in trout. From a couple of feet below the surface, it must look like the bug is about to take off and become a missed opportunity. Strikes are usually strong enough to allow me to get my eight-year-old son to do the honors of hooking the fish.

Getting Wet

You'll undoubtedly find a time when fish are rising everywhere except directly under your fly. You change dry-fly patterns, running the gamut from size 12 Elk Hair Caddis to size 20 Griffith's Gnat, all without results. It can be the most frustrating of angling experiences, but don't fling your rod into the deep water. Chances are that the trout are taking emerging insects a couple of inches under the surface or in the surface film itself. It's a perfect opportunity to try out the time-honored, often-neglected class of flies—the wets.

We were camped in a basin of eight high lakes in Wyoming, exquisite gems strung on a thread of sparkling water. After a restless night spent huddled in a tent, the nylon rippling all night under the strain of fierce winds, I was up at first light, tired of lying in my bag wide awake. The wind had calmed, and the sun promised to burn through the clouds before too long, so I grabbed my rod and left a sleeping camp behind. To my delight, the resident brook trout had risen early, too, and seemed to be feeding readily on some small bugs I couldn't quite see. "No matter," as I always think, "it's mountain water, and they'll take my fly."

An hour later I'd lost that magical sunrise mood and was feeling as foul as the weather. I had clung to mountain-water rules and the fish were laughing at my inflexibility.

I sat on a rock and snapped open my fly box. At home, and under the influence of Dave Hughes's great work *Wet Flies*, I'd been wise enough to follow the advice of a master and throw in a couple of the odd-looking flymphs and more easy-to-accept soft hackles that he had spent 40,000 words praising. Knowing Dave, he couldn't be leading me far astray when he wrote that these things could work on lakes.

"What the hell," I said out loud as I tied on a glob of fur that Dave had credited to Pete Hidy and called a "flymph." I dropped the fly into the water at my feet to get it wet enough to sink below the surface an inch or two, and while it was there, I marveled at its action when I gave the line a little tug. With a loosely wound body and those long, soft dun hackles, the fly pulsed through the water with a motion that had to be an exact copy of a swimming insect.

The results were immediate. Brookie after brookie took the tiny olive flymph as I dragged it just below the surface. It worked so well I felt guilty, like I suddenly had an unfair advantage over the trout.

Whenever dry flies fail to lure a strike on a lake, I turn to soft hackles or flymphs. In most cases, the patterns imitate caddis flies or other aquatic insects that are making their way to the surface to hatch. A slow, stop-and-start retrieve of such a fly just below the surface can produce what seems like a miracle.

Cast your fly in the vicinity of rising fish. Wait a couple of seconds, then pull back slightly on the rod tip to set the fly in motion. Tighten the line a bit with your nonrod hand, then begin to strip the line a couple of inches at time. Be ready to set the hook, which you should do whenever you feel a tug on the line.

I tie my flymphs on stout wet-fly hooks to ensure that they will sink when they hit the surface film. You can vary the depth that you begin the retrieve by changing how you grease the tippet. If you want the flymph to scoot along near the surface, apply floatant to all but the last 6 inches of the tippet; to go deeper, leave more of the tippet ungreased.

My soft hackles are put on two types of hooks. The heavier wet-fly hooks help the pattern sink a bit as with the flymphs, and you can use the same tippet techniques to add a little variation to the way the fly is presented. I also put some soft hackles on dry-fly hooks. When these hit the surface, they don't readily sink, but a tug on the line will usually drop them just through the surface film. Using the strip retrieve, these "dry" soft hackles come along just below the surface, and at times it is this technique that wins over the fish.

Soft hackles are easy patterns to tie, so I have quite a few of them in my lake box. While olive- and yellow-bodied patterns seem the most effective, you'll find orange, gray, and red patterns in my box, too. I try to carry two flies of each color and hook style from size 12 down to size 16. I can't seem to manage getting a decent partridge feather on anything smaller. For flymphs, though, I carry a couple of each size down to size 18. It's hard to justify carrying anything other than olive-bodied flymphs to high lakes, but I always throw in some Hare's Ear Flymphs and Pale Watery Wingless Flymphs just in case I feel like experimenting.

It's not always possible to time your visit to an alpine lake for the morning or evening rise. The trails to plenty of lakes make it impossible for mere mortals to sling a heavy pack there. A 2-hour hike from base camp usually puts me at a high lake as the morning hatches are ending, so my time is spent staring at a featureless surface with no sign of trout. Fortunately, the fish are still there and are willing to accommodate you if you have some patience and are willing to work a little harder.

When nothing is stirring, I find success in fishing streamers around whatever structure the lake has to offer. It's definitely time to seek out the talus slopes or the rockiest shoreline. Chances are, there are plenty of good fish sitting around in the protection offered by the rocks, and they will be willing to sample a big enough morsel if it swims by. Fly-pattern selection won't be critical here—standards like black and olive Woolly Buggers are all you need.

When you've found the hidden structure along the bottom and shore of the lake, you'll have to find a way to present your fly pattern as close to the bottom rocks as possible. Use weighted streamers, and if you can't feel the bottom when you're fishing, you might want a little extra weight on the leader a foot or so up from the fly. Make a long cast out from the shore and let the fly sink. You want to strip the fly along the bottom, then up the shelf to the shore. If you are fishing deep water, count to twenty before beginning your retrieve. Not on the bottom yet? Wait longer before bringing the fly toward you. Vary the strip rate and the depth until you start to find fish. Remember, here's one time when patience is required.

The trout of high-country lakes are like your eccentric uncle—they are just so hard to accurately predict. No matter how much effort or thought you put into fishing there, some days on some lakes are going to be fantastic, while others—and this is by far more often the case—will test your skills to the utmost.

High lakes can test your patience in another way. This past summer, I couldn't wait to get into the high lakes of the South San Juan Wilderness, and I plotted a Fourth of July trip to Lake Ann just below the Continental Divide. Six miles of thin air were laced with the anticipation of making that first cast—a cast that never came. As I finally stepped up over the moraine that dammed the lake, I saw that the surface was completely frozen.

Don't rush a trip into lake country, but learn to determine when ice-out occurs on your favorite spots. I've found that it takes a few trips, or at least talking to the right anglers, to figure when ice-out usually occurs. In normal years, the type that never seem to come anymore, ice-out occurs on lakes around 12,000 feet in late June or early July in Colorado. Go north to Wyoming or Montana, however, and you have to wait until late July to fish lakes at 10,000 feet. I've been to Wyoming lakes still covered with ice in late August, so here is a case where there's a lot of variation. Warm spring temperatures bring on ice-out earlier, and cold years can delay the coming of open water.

If you're lucky or skilled enough to time it right, ice-out is a great time to fish a lake. The fish are hungry, the insects are hatching, and the solitude is divine. Cast as close to the ice line as you can. Mayflies are great little patterns to use in this situation. Another effective technique is to cast terrestrials—flying ants or beetles—onto the ice, then give the line a tug to pop the pattern off the ice and onto the water.

Dam Beavers

No treatment of fishing high-country stillwater would be complete without some mention of beaver ponds. But I must admit, these brief interruptions of small-stream flow aren't really for the casual fly fisher. Combine their restricted surface area, their clear water, the surrounding willows, and the smart trout, and you've got a challenge that is worthy of the most experienced angler.

If you apply strict mountain-water rules to beaver ponds, you'll probably come away mumbling about the tiny brookies you caught. Mountain-water rules say that you should take pleasure in those tiny trout, but with a little care, you can find pleasure in a couple of big ones, too. Indeed, beaver ponds are home to plenty of small brookies, but with a little careful consideration, you can find one of the bigger trout that almost always ply the waters behind dams of sticks and mud.

On the simplest level, you can look at beaver ponds as tiny lakes. Most ponds, in fact, aren't much more than a single cast in diameter. But you'll have to add a large dose of caution to your technique when you fish such a small, confined area. A single misplaced cast, a heavy footfall, or a torso silhouette will disturb the workings of the entire pond and chase the trout into hiding. Before you fish a pond, think stealth. You have to be plain sneaky to catch a good-sized trout in a beaver pond.

Figure that, just like in a lake, the best fish will be in deep water near structure. Beavers usually build their dams on flats in meadows or in thin woodlands, far removed from rocky cliffs. Not many boulders show up in the ponds to provide cover for trout, so they find it elsewhere—in submerged logs, waterlogged tree roots, overhanging vegetation, along the dam, or in the old stream channel where the water is a bit deeper than other spots in the pond.

The trick is to spot the structure without showing yourself to the fish in the pond. You must maintain a low profile near a beaver pond or every trout living there will head for the hills. Don't approach the open banks while upright. Kneel or crawl if necessary. Better still, stay far back from the shore and glean what you can of the hidden features of the pond. Keeping your distance also helps avoid sending out ground vibrations that the muck surrounding the ponds can broadcast into the water, where the message will be clear to the inhabitants.

You can use brushy-stream tactics successfully on some beaver ponds, using vegetation as cover and dapping a fly on the water. Occasionally you'll find a nice trout that is willing to take a dry fly this way, but since most pond trout feed below the surface, you want to find ways to work a nymph. Cross-country casts, like those you use on meadow streams, can get a nymph out into the portions of the pond you want to work. Kneel back from the bank as far as you can, and cast so that the fly line lands on the ground and only the leader, tippet, and fly hit the water. Your target should be off to the side of where you expect to find a trout. You can't just let the nymph sit there and expect the fish to do all the work. Let the pattern sink a few seconds, then twitch your nymph past the structure to which you are casting. Go slowly, taking care not to disturb the surface too much. It's a tense kind of angling that is also pretty exciting.

Probably the best approach to many beaver ponds is to fish over the dam. The dam will effectively screen you from the view of the trout. You only need to have your head above the dam to check out the place without exposing yourself to the fish. You must use some care in managing your line well to avoid getting tangled in the sticks of the dam. Like in swift-water stream angling, a good solution here is to use your arm as an extension of your fly rod. After you make a cast, hold your rod a bit over the level of your head and point it at the pond. It's an awkward position, but it keeps you and your rod mostly out of sight of the pond. When a fish strikes, you must be careful to lift quickly upward with your wrist.

As on lakes, you'll find that beaver-pond angling is best when the light isn't direct and bright. Morning and evenings are good, but cloudy afternoons can bring on the best feeding times. Let a little breeze from a nearby thunderstorm ripple the surface of the pond, and you'll find that conditions for catching the pond's prize aren't quite so tough. When the storm arrives and it doesn't come down in sheets of rain, keep fishing, and you'll find that the trout aren't quite so much on their guard.

One last caution on beaver ponds—they are the most ephemeral of mountain features. Those that are shown on a topographic map are usually long gone by the time the map is printed. Ponds with a long-standing reputation will be silted in by the time you get there. I've had a trusted acquaintance entice me in June with the praises of two particular ponds, but I couldn't make the hike until fall. I found one pond to be a mud hole as thick as a mocha milkshake, and the other was completely washed out by the summer's rains. The only reliable way to find good beaver-pond fishing is to explore the high meadows whenever you are there.

Chapter Nine

Finding New Water

My friends call me the Mapmeister. In addition to the unruly pile that clutters my desk, I have file cabinets and dresser drawers filled with maps—topographic maps on three scales, national-forest maps, geologic maps, road maps, and statewide atlases. They are neatly sorted by type of map, state, and region. I keep a supply in the bathroom in lieu of magazines. On many, you'll find a couple out-of-the-way streams highlighted in blue. These are the places I've only dreamed about, ones that remain but a blue line on a map, never explored.

For anglers just as intent on exploring as they are on catching fish, maps are the most valuable resource for finding your own little piece of mountain water. They'll show you spots on well-known rivers that others may overlook and streams that are hard to get to but that hold long meadows that get fished maybe twice a year. Maps make you curious about a string of ponds in a high valley and help you find lakes that are far from the nearest trail. For me, maps are as much a part of armchair angling in front of the burning piñon logs as are the writings of Gierach and Holt. Maps can hold my interest throughout the winter, enticing me with visions of the summer to come and high places to check out.

Although I get teased for having enough maps to give triplicate or quadruple coverage of an area, each type of map provides a piece of information vital to the success of an exploratory fishing trip. A simple road map will get you within striking distance of a new stream or lake, but a new collection of large-scale state road atlases is immensely more helpful. Atlases such as those produced by DeLorme Mapping show not only the main and secondary roads, but topography, details of watersheds, land ownership, and campgrounds—all information that is essential for a successful trip to waters near the roads. Most angling in the mountains is found in the national forests, and maps produced by the U.S. Forest Service supplement road maps with a breakdown of the quality of the road surface, be it paved, gravel, dirt, or four-wheel-drive track. These colorful maps also make it easy to spot in a glance whether or not your destination is on public land.

Yes, its fanatical, but I've been know to consult geologic maps before heading out to a new spot. The most colorful of all maps, these charts detail the underlying rock structure of the mountains. Why would this ever be important in trip planning? Certain types of rock, notably granites and metamorphic rocks like gneiss, are hard rocks that produce clean streambeds and clear water. Other rocks such as shale erode into clay and silt that often cover the bottom of a stream or, at the very least, produce a turbid flow following the slightest rainstorm. Notorious in these parts is the Mancos shale, a rock layer that spreads from northern New Mexico to northern Colorado. It's the source of the many streams in the area that are named Rio Blanco, "White River," because the clay from the shale washes into the streams and produces a milky flow that makes for poor angling. During summer rainy spells, I avoid any stream that flows through

Mancos shale, saving it for weeks when the skies and the water are clear.

Geologic maps are attractive, with interlocking bands of color to represent different rock types. With a little practice, you can learn to read the story written in the bedrock and apply it to your angling explorations. It doesn't take long to discover which of your local rocks make for fine angling and which may produce difficult conditions. In general, granite, limestone, gneiss, basalt (hardened lava flows), and other well-glued rock types offer the best chances for clean streams and streambeds. Poorly cemented sedimentary rocks—sandstone, shale, and mudstone—and air-fall deposits from volcanoes (usually called tuff or pumice) create conditions for murky streams that turn to café au lait after modest rains. Geologic maps are available from local map stores, from state offices of mining and mineral resources, and from the United States Geological Survey (USGS). Check out the USGS on the World Wide Web (www.usgs.gov) for the names of available maps.

When you are looking beyond the roads for a backcountry angling adventure, the large scale of USGS 7.5-minute topographic quadrangle maps is an essential tool for navigation and personal safety. Topographic maps are like treasure maps that show the location of streams and lakes and the trails that will take you there. If there isn't an established route to the water, the contour lines of the map will let you figure out the path of least resistance to your secret destination. With a bit of skill in map reading, the charts will also let you guess a few of the characteristics of the water you seek. Of course, none of this will work if you don't possess the fundamental ability to read a map, to work with a compass, or to program a Global Positioning Satellite (GPS) system receiving unit.

In a nutshell, topographic maps show the lay of the land. Green areas are forested, and white areas are open country. Details of roads and streams cut across the basic background of color. The most useful features of the maps are the brown contour lines. Each continuous line represents a single elevation; if you could walk one of the lines on the ground, you would never head uphill or downhill. Crossing lines is when you have to work hard, and the closer the lines are together, the steeper the hill. Some lines are spaced at 20-foot intervals, others at 40 feet. Remember that streams and lakes always lie at the bottom of hills, and peaks, which are usually labeled as such or are shown as a series of tight concentric loops, are the high ground. Find a stream enclosed in widely spaced contour lines and you're in for an easy walk into the valley; when the lines are squeezed together into brown swirls, the valley is protected by cliffs.

In the real world, maps are meant to be used in connection with a compass or with the GPS system. I find that on a clear day, a map is enough to get me where I want to go and back to my truck. I use the terrain and the map to navigate, and I have learned from my mistakes and *never* go anywhere off the trail without the topo sheet for the area. I've rarely used a compass to navigate. I'm usually heading for the long line of a stream or a road and know that I will eventually hit it if I walk a reasonably straight line. If your destination is a point—a lake, a pass, or your car—a compass and map can be a real plus in getting to the right spot.

I am a sucker for technology, and I've gone the lazy route to navigation and use a GPS when my destination is a point. Using military satellites, the GPS can tell me my location to within 100 meters, and with a map and clear day, that's usually enough to tell exactly where I am. I can also tell the receiver to remember the location of my truck and thus can use the unit to guide me back without a lot of fuss. A GPS isn't infallible, but it does make off-trail travel a bit safer.

Put it all together and you can spot a neglected stream from the comfort of your favorite chair. Use the map to figure out the trails that lead to the stream or lake, how far you'll have to walk, and, if you're headed out overnight, maybe where you can expect to find a campsite. You'll be able to find a way to reach the stream when it swings away from the trail and spots that tend to see little angling pressure.

Detailed topographic maps can be useful even to the angler who doesn't want a long hike. You can use the map to spot locations on popular water near roads that might not see as many anglers as the areas adjacent to the road. I'm looking at a map of the Conejos River in southern Colorado and remembering how I used it to find the biggest brown trout I ever hooked in the mountains. The road that follows the entire course of the lower river runs a fairly straight line through the canyon, but the river turns through loops and half-circles and in a few spots swings as much as a half-mile away from the road. One such bend grabbed my attention. Downstream is a popular campground, and I figured that most anglers would start there and work upstream maybe a quarter-mile or a half-mile. Upstream from the bend in question, the river stays within sight of the road. In between was a mile-long swing that pushed as far from the road as the valley allowed, and much of the river was shielded from view of the road by a low ridge. Indeed, when I reached my destination, there were no boot prints in the mud, no beer cans on the banks, and no fishing line hanging from the trees like Christmas tinsel. When I stepped back from the water, I was within earshot of the cars on the road, but by the size of the trout in that bend, I'd guess that not more than a dozen anglers a year stumbled onto the fertile stretch.

Use maps to look for spots on more popular rivers that are hard to reach. Sections that lie back from the road are an obvious choice, but places that require a bit of a climb to get back to your car are often surprisingly barren of anglers. On the little Rio San Antonio near my home, the sections of the

Using Maps to Find New Water

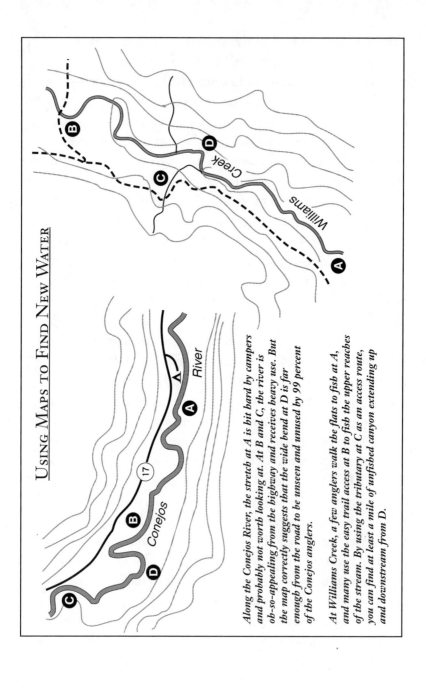

Along the Conejos River, the stretch at A is bit hard by campers and probably not worth looking at. At B and C, the river is ob-so-appealing from the highway and receives heavy use. But the map correctly suggests that the wide bend at D is far enough from the road to be unseen and unused by 99 percent of the Conejos anglers.

At Williams Creek, a few anglers walk the flats to fish at A, and many use the easy trail access at B to fish the upper reaches of the stream. By using the tributary at C as an access route, you can find at least a mile of unfished canyon extending up and downstream from D.

stream at road level get hit hard, but the pocket water in the reaches that lie 200 feet below the road surface rarely attract the casual angler and thus hold some decent trout. Stay at least a quarter-mile away from public campgrounds—that water gets hit hard. You can often use maps to locate little sections of water on public land that are sandwiched upstream and downstream by private holdings. If you try such a spot, make sure that you can read a map well enough to stay on public land.

Maps will not only tell you where the water is located but will give you an idea of the type of water you'll find there. The spacing of the contour lines tells you the gradient of the stream. A river crossing over closely spaced contour lines means a high gradient, and you can expect to find some foaming pocket water filled with cascades and plunge pools. Also, look at the vegetation symbols. In a narrow canyon that lacks the green shading of forest there will probably be bouldery water. Where contour lines are more widely spaced, the water will be flatter. You can judge the size of the stream from the size of the watershed above the point that interests you. Look at the area of land drained and the number of tributaries that feed it.

It's not always easy to tell which streams or lakes will hold fish and which ones will be barren. Tributaries of rivers important enough to have a name probably hold fish. Look for waterfalls—concentrations of brown lines across the stream—and figure that the reach below the falls will hold fish. In the southern Rockies, most lakes up to 12,000 feet will have populations of trout, but in the north, I haven't seen many lakes higher than 10,500 feet that are worth fishing.

Finding a quiet lake is a bit more problematic. There aren't as many lakes as streams to go around, and even fewer are reachable by trail. One thing you'll find is that social trails will take you to most of the lakes that don't have maintained trails leading to them, which makes the trip a little easier. It's almost impossible to look at a map and tell which lake will hold fish and which will be barren. On more than one occasion, I've made the 2,000-foot climb to a lake only to find it fishless. Such is the nature of exploring—win some, lose some. Yet, you don't want to overlook any lake at a reasonable elevation. Sometimes the smallest, most obscure tarn lakes hold surprisingly good trout.

When you're perusing your maps in front of the fireplace, the ideal situation is to locate a stream that flows perpendicular to a dirt road and that has a trail paralleling it along the slopes above. This situation gives you a couple of advantages if you're looking to find water that doesn't see a lot of other anglers. The stream heads away from the nearest road, and anyone who fishes there will have to walk in. That eliminates 90 percent of the competition. If you walk the trail above the stream at least a half-mile from the road, you'll cut out 50 percent of the remaining anglers. Because the stream and trail are separated, the rest of the anglers are dispersed—not everyone will cut down from the trail at the same spot. If the stream in question is a couple of miles long, you're more than likely to find a spot that hasn't been fished all season.

The most exciting new maps in my collection aren't made of paper but of magnetic dots on a CD-ROM. Computerized topographic maps are increasingly available and affordable. The data on a single CD can cover a tenth of a large western state, about the area of 100 7.5-minute topographic quadrangle maps. The price comes out to be much less on disk, and what these maps lack in convenience they make up for in additional features. You can create and print custom maps for a specific trip, electronically plot your route directly on the printout, and generate a profile of the route to accurately portray the elevation gain and loss of your trip.

Rugged canyons that require a hike to get to offer solitary angling at its finest.

The easiest (but admittedly the least fun) method of scouting new water is to let someone else do the work and buy a guidebook to the area you are interested in exploring. Many authors have tried to cover an entire state, but the trend to regional guides is a boon to the angler who wants to explore. You'll get the basics about a small area, and you'll feel in touch with mountain rhythms, if the author did his job well.

Guidebook writers are frequently accused of spilling the beans, giving away secrets for money. I've written a few guidebooks, and I can tell you that there isn't a whole lot of cash to be made in that business. That's not the point, however, and I don't think the majority of guidebook authors are in it to make even a small killing. I believe that most guidebook writers are like myself—born to teach—and a book is one way to accomplish that. Before I turned to writing, I taught about the natural world in public schools, nature centers, museums, and national parks. Creating a guidebook to fly fishing was a natural extension of my passion for helping others learn. Other guidebook authors cite a strong desire to protect wild-trout fisheries as their primary motivation for writing.

Guidebooks are there to help you get started on the quest to new water. Use the author's suggestions to get started, but don't stop where the words end. Use the guide to push a bit farther. Chances are, even the author hasn't explored beyond what is written about in detail, or if he has, he's not telling you more for selfish reasons, trying to keep a stretch or two out of the public eye.

Don't forget word of mouth as a source of information about new streams. Hang out at the local fly-fishing shop. Find a nearby angling club and attend its meetings. These clubs usually have programs put on by local guides who discuss their favorite waters—places that they have the time and motivation to seek out for their clients. Or you can hire a guide who is willing to take you to a more remote location to fish.

Goin' Where the Other Guy Ain't

Mountain-water rules don't work very well on the heavily fished waters of Yellowstone National Park. The glassy surface of Biscuit Basin on the Firehole River is the kind of place all the other angling authors talk about—the monster trout won't move for an imitation that isn't dressed as impeccably as Tom Cruise at the Oscars, without a hair out of place. But that doesn't mean you can't find a memorable fish in the park without all that attention to detail.

A family vacation isn't the time for serious fly fishing in Yellowstone—too many appointments with spouting geysers, road-blocking bison, and early-morning wolf-watching sessions. I had a half an hour here and there to escape to the streams and, of course, I wanted to be able to name drop when I got home. So I'd pull off the road along the Firehole, the Lamar, and the Madison. Thirty minutes is barely enough time to rig a rod and make a few futile casts. In my frustration, I was dealing more with knots, tangles, and the wrong time of day than with rising fish. I was anxious for the chance to wrestle a good trout.

On the third day, I drove past the heartbreakingly beautiful scenes of Elk Park and Gibbon Meadows—places that were as concentrated with anglers as the Hayden Valley was with bison—and headed for some classic mountain water. I spotted a long string of riffles and pockets below Gibbon Falls, water where I knew I wouldn't have to finesse any trout. The family deposited for a rest on a sandy beach, I dashed downstream for my half-hour of angling time.

The water slid toward the Firehole, not in sweeping meanders, but in hops and jumps, interrupted by several deep runs containing huge submerged rocks. In contrast to the sandbars along the Lamar and Firehole, there were no felt-soled footprints punched amid the raccoon and elk tracks on the wet banks. Studying the currents, I instantly found two dozen likely spots to cast a fly.

It was mountain water at its finest—turbulent, interesting, and unfished. I immediately felt comfortable, alert, and confident.

After two dozen casts and a couple of small browns, I was ready to try the sweet spot—the deepest, least choppy run. Casting from behind a log burned in the 1988 fires, I threw a size 10 Royal Wulff into the current tongue. The familiar, quick rise of a brown snatching a morsel from a fast current followed. The heavy pull was startling, and I was certain that my 5X tippet and my hurriedly tied knots would give way as the trout cranked out line from my reel, heading upstream. Working gingerly, I eased the brown in, cursing myself for using such light tippet. When I cradled him tenderly in my hands, the 4-pound trout reached a hair past the San Juan mark on my rod.

I had found true mountain water in Yellowstone, and I was content to hustle upstream and rejoin the tourist crowds.

I've been an admirer of Henry David Thoreau ever since I read his words in *Walden:* "I would rather sit on a pumpkin and have it all to myself, than be crowded on a velvet cushion." It's my nature to want a solitary stream experience, and I think the vast majority of other anglers feel that way. I usually refuse to fish when another angler is in sight. Whenever I hit the water, I want the illusion that the river is mine for a day. Thus, I am constantly in search of spots that I'm certain will be devoid of human life except for my own.

On mountain streams and lakes, with a bit of forethought and timing, you can find that stretch of water that is all your own. It takes patience and a bit of walking, but the effort will pay huge dividends at the end of the day when you come away feeling all smoothed out.

The first method of finding your own stretch of water is to avoid those seductive reaches of stream that others can't pass by. Pretty places with running water visible from a road or trail will act like a magnet to attract anglers. Most anglers have to fish the gentle-flowing meadow waters, and they concentrate in these spots. If you put in the effort to walk upstream or downstream into the adjacent canyons, you are almost guaranteed solitude on any stream.

Put some distance between yourself and the road. You've undoubtedly heard the 10-90 rule of fishing—the one that says 10 percent of the anglers catch 90 percent of the fish. I've heard a variation of the rule that speaks to the search for open water: If you walk 10 minutes from the road, you'll leave behind 90 percent of the anglers. It's a reasonable statement, but not enough for my liking. The six-pack rule is perhaps better for those seeking solitude: Walk away from the

If you are willing to strap on a backpack and put a few miles between you and your car, the mountains will offer miles of solitary angling.

road until you pick up six beer cans, then start fishing. Either way you want to go, the idea is clear—you have to get away from the road to hit true mountain water.

I admit it's not an easy thing, however, to pass up decent-looking runs when you're anxious to start fishing. It takes some discipline, and you really have to establish your plan before you start walking or else you'll be sucked down to the water before you really want to be. You also need to train yourself to walk right by the spots that everyone else thinks look like terrific holes. Deep, slow-moving pools on mountain streams inevitably attract every angler who walks by, and you can count the number of spinners hanging from the surrounding trees to prove it. Walk by those lovely meadow stretches that attract a crowd, then hit the pocket water above.

Another consideration in western mountains is the slope factor. This works for streams that run through reasonably deep canyons and that have a trail leading up the canyon. In the old days, the trail up the canyon stayed close to the stream, but to prevent erosion directly into the water, modern trail-building methods have moved most trails up the slope, considerably above the canyon bottom. You can always find some reasonably unfished water in such a place. You know that the first half-mile above the trailhead gets hit hard, so walk upstream on the trail at least that far. Then put the slope factor into play. Most anglers will drop to the stream in the spots where the trail and stream converge. So look for spots where the trail is far above the stream and the slope leading down to it is steep. You can usually find a place where you can safely switchback across a vegetated slope—don't go charging straight down a rocky hillside—and reach the stream in a few minutes. You'll often find very few signs of recent use by other anglers, and you'll have a long section of river to yourself.

Like anyone else, anglers are creatures of habit, and they have a strong tendency to treat fly fishing like anything else, indulging in the sport when it is most convenient for them. As a result, streams are most crowded in the middle of the day, regardless of hatches, weather, or water temperature. It's simply the easiest time of day to wet a line, working around schedules, meals, and the need to be someplace else. If you break the pattern, you're more likely to find the river empty.

On one of my rare days on the San Juan River below Navajo Dam, I was disgusted by the midday crowds, especially up near the dam where catch-and-release regulations concentrate huge rainbows. Veteran San Juan angler Hugo Ableson entreated me to put away my displeasure and hang around awhile, promising a real treat. He was right. At 4 P.M. he took me up to the dam—where just a few hours before, bewadered anglers were lined up like trout at a lake inlet—and we fished for 3 hours in utter solitude, wrestling monster rainbows until our arms ached.

This overlooked stretch of the Frying Pan River is only a few steps away from a state highway.

If you want to avoid other anglers, plan to fish early or late in the day. If the stream isn't too high in elevation, be on the water by 8:30 A.M. There will be a few bugs over the surface and trout will be feeding, and you won't be competing with other rods for the best holes. The same holds true for the two hours before sunset. It's incomprehensible to me why so many anglers head home just when the action is picking up. In the evening, insects are more active, water temperatures are at their highest level of the day, and the sun is off the water, enticing trout to feed. So plan your mountain-water day around angling in the evening. Take an afternoon hike, have a bowl of soup at 4 P.M., hit the water by 5 P.M., and enjoy fishing until you can't see well enough to change flies.

Ask ten anglers from around these parts their favorite month to go fly fishing, and nine of them will answer September or

October. The pinch of coolness in the air, the quality of light, and the aspens glowing on the mountainsides are only partially responsible for this bent. There is far less competition on the water once the kids are back in school. It's another way anglers are ruled by the clock: Labor Day is deemed the end of summer and thus must be the end of the fishing season. If you seek solitude, you're certain to find it in the fall.

The same effects of habit are found on the other end of the season. Many anglers won't think about fishing until July, but pre-runoff fly fishing can be fun. Here, timing is everything, and you have to know your local rivers well to catch them when water temperatures are rising and the flow volume isn't. Another way to play off the early season to catch an empty stream is to use a mountain bike to reach waters located on roads blocked to vehicles by snow.

Is it worth the effort? Fishing a mile of stream or a speck of a lake and having it all to yourself is the essence of mountain water.

Stream of Consciousness

The Rio Vallecitos looked like my kind of place—a narrow canyon with clear, cold water, a smattering of mayflies, and rising wild trout. My first cast with a Parachute Adams met with a gaping mouth of a trout, and a surprising number of other offerings met the same fate. The river endlessly beckoned, each bend offering a delightful prospect and every reach holding a hundred trout lies.

The roll of thunder off the hills brought me out of a spell. "Early in the day for a shower," I thought, glancing at my watch. Three o'clock! No wonder my arm ached and the hole in my stomach was screaming for food. I'd been fishing for six hours, yet it seemed I had just started. I was in fly-fishing nirvana.

Nirvana. There it goes again, another link between fly fishing and spirituality. Although angler authors from Maclean to Gierach speak of fly fishing in terms of religion, I never figured out exactly what about the sport coupled the two. Just what had put me in that state of bliss?

While casting a Parachute Adams between the rocks of the Vallecitos, I had stopped talking to myself. Normally, the little voice inside my head is as incessant as the stream-of-consciousness ramblings of my three-year-old son, yet it serves no useful purpose. On the river, the voice was silent, I lived on pure instinct, and time was almost nonexistent, passing unnoticed like the wing beats of a mayfly.

The trancelike state of mind happens every time I am on mountain water. When I arrive, I quickly focus on the trout's environment. I am aware of the time of day and the season, and I process information on water clarity and temperature. I estimate depths, picture the shape of the unseen stream bottom, and guess which rocks might deflect enough of the current to make life comfortable for a trout. Based on where a trout might lie and how my fly will ride on the water, I pick a location to cast my fly.

The amazing thing about this full palette of observation and inference is that none of it happens with the higher brain. Such complex, interrelated decisions should clutter the mind with thoughts, but the process is just the opposite—it simply happens. After years of trial and error, the details of catching trout on a high-mountain stream become instinctual. Observation of the environment is translated directly into action. No internal dialogue is required.

All the religions teach the importance of striving for a oneness with God or the Universe. Most center attention on shutting off the outside world, focusing on a single thought or object, and withdrawing inside oneself. It is like what happens during my other outdoor pursuits. When running, cross-country skiing, mountain biking, or hiking, regular deep drafts of air and the staccato rhythms of my moving feet overpower all else, forcing me inside myself. The voice is louder than ever.

Only fly fishing silences the internal dialogue. The secret lies not within myself, but in the opposite direction—flood the senses with a complete, detailed picture of the world. By total immersion into the trout environment—mayflies, water depth, stream architecture—I not only stop the constant conversation in my brain, but seem to become a part of my surroundings. Standing at midstream, the trout's fluid home pressing against my feet and legs, totally concentrating on the river, yet completely relaxed, I meld into the trout's world.

The underlying meanings of fly fishing make actually catching a trout less important than the act itself. Simply spending time in a place where trout live and experiencing the world directly, without talking to myself for a couple of hours, brings deep satisfaction, and that is enough to take home. When I do fool a trout, I have no choice but to release it back to the water. As I come to feel more a part of the trout's environment, why would I want to kill a part of myself?

INDEX